BAYVIEW HIGH

THE BIG SPLIT

H.A. Levigne

Vanwell Publishing Limited
St. Catharines, Ontario

Vanwell Publishing acknowledges the financial support of the
Government of Canada through the Book Publishing Industry
Development Program for our publishing activities.

Vanwell Publishing acknowledges the Government of Ontario
through the Ontario Media Development Corporation's Book
Initiative.

Vanwell Publishing Limited
P.O. Box 2131
1 Northrup Crescent
St. Catharines, ON
Canada L2R 7S2
sales@vanwell.com
1-800-661-6136

Produced and designed by Tea Leaf Press Inc.
www.tealeafpress.com

Printed in Canada

National Library of Canada Cataloguing in Publication

Levigne, Heather, 1974–
    The big split / H.A. Levigne.

(Bayview High, ISSN 1702-0174)
ISBN 1-55068-117-6

    I. Divorce—Juvenile fiction. I. Title II. Series.

PS8573.E96438B44 2003   jC813'.6   C2003-905509-4

For my dad,
who is always there for me

chapter 1

happy birthday

Zack heard the back door swing open and then slam shut. He pulled his head out of the deep freeze and pushed his sandy blond hair out of his eyes. *That must be Mom,* he thought. *Good.* He had been trying to fit two big bags of ice into the freezer for the past half-hour. Of course, they wouldn't fit.

Zack walked to the kitchen doorway, flexing his numb fingers. His mother was crouching in front of the fridge. Her head was stuck halfway inside. Zack watched for a moment as she stacked cans of soda. Bags of groceries lay on the floor all around her. "Zack! Did you get the ice?" she asked without looking at him.

"Yeah, but it won't fit in the stupid freezer," Zack said. "Come and see for yourself."

His mother followed him back to the freezer. She looked around. Frozen food lay all over the floor. Zack had pulled it out of the freezer to make room for the ice. A large tub of chocolate ice cream was beginning to melt. With a sigh, Mrs. Brown began to put things back.

"Zack, can you get the hot dogs and buns ready for the barbecue? People are going to be here any minute," Mrs. Brown said.

"All right," said Zack. It was his little sister Shellie's sixth birthday. They were having a party for her. His mother had even hired a clown for the afternoon.

Zack's mom handed him a few cans of frozen lemonade. Somehow, she fit the rest of the food back into the freezer. "There! Bring that lemonade with you." Mrs. Brown turned and walked back to the kitchen. Zack followed her.

"Where's Dad?" he asked, putting the lemonade in the sink to thaw. He pulled out a stool and sat down at the counter. A tray of frosted cupcakes for the party sat nearby. Mrs. Brown bent down to finish putting the rest of the food in the fridge. Zack sneaked a cupcake off the tray while her back was turned.

"He had to go into the office for a few hours. Oh, that reminds me. I'd better call and remind him to pick up the cake on the way home. Put that cupcake back, please," Mrs. Brown said without turning around.

Zack frowned and put it back. "He had to work *today?* Couldn't he at least take the day off for Shellie's party?"

"He's closing a sale on a house," Mrs. Brown replied as she dialed Mr. Brown's cell phone. "He should be home soon."

Zack's father was a real estate agent. Lately, he had been working pretty long hours. He was hardly ever home in time for dinner these days. He seemed to be at work all the time. Zack couldn't remember the last time they had gone to a ball game. Even though he was seventeen, he still liked to hang out with his dad now and then. They always had a good time. Zack would not admit it to anyone, but he kind of missed spending time with his dad.

Mrs. Brown's face became more and more annoyed as she waited for Mr. Brown to pick up his cell phone. Finally, she said, "Andrew, it's Denise. Where are you?"

She was silent for a moment as she listened to Zack's dad. Zack watched the expression on his mother's face grow angrier.

"Are you telling me you won't be here at *all?*" she asked in disbelief. "Andrew, what am I supposed to tell Shellie?"

Zack frowned. He knew what that meant. His mother was going to expect *him* to stay and help with the party. He couldn't think of a worse way to spend a sunny Sunday afternoon.

Mrs. Brown hung up the phone and turned to Zack. "I need you to stick around and help me with the party," she said. Her face was red and angry. She yanked packages of plastic cups and paper plates from the cupboards.

"Aw, Mom, I don't want to hang around a bunch of little kids all day. I was going to go out with Heidi," Zack complained. His girlfriend, Heidi, was off work that afternoon. She had to work almost every Sunday. She was free today, though. *And now I'm not,* Zack thought bitterly. *Thanks a lot, Dad.*

The doorbell rang loudly. "Darn! I still have to finish making a salad," Mrs. Brown said with a glance at the clock. "Zack, go and answer the door for me please."

"I thought you wanted me to get the hot dogs and buns ready," Zack muttered. *I'm definitely not staying all day,* he thought. He stopped at the doorway and turned around. "What about the cake?" he asked his mother.

Mrs. Brown stopped in her tracks. She looked horrified. "Oh, no! Your father was supposed to bring it!" She looked at her watch.

"I don't have time to go and get one." Her eyes fell on Zack.

"No way," he said, shaking his head. "I'll stay and help, but I'm not going to pick up some stupid pink cake." He pointed at the tray of cupcakes. "Why don't you just stick a candle in one of those?"

Mrs. Brown glanced at the cupcakes. She frowned. Then she nodded. "Yes, I suppose they'll do." She was still banging cupboard doors when Zack walked out.

chapter 2

brothers and sisters

Zack opened the front door to find a little girl with bright red hair standing there. She gave him a gap-toothed grin. In her arms she held a box wrapped in colorful paper. "Hi, Zack! This is for Shellie! It's a skipping rope that lights up! Guess what? I lost my front tooth today! And the tooth fairy gave me two dollars for it! And—"

"Okay, Suzy. Why don't we go out to the backyard?" said the woman standing behind her. She led her daughter past him. Zack had just put the gift in the living room when the doorbell rang again. He played doorman for the next half hour as people arrived for the party.

Zack began to move the pile of presents from the living room to the deck behind the house. Just then, the doorbell rang again.

"Go home. The party's over," he said under his breath as he opened the door.

"No way! I want some cake," said the pretty, brown-haired girl standing on the porch. Her green eyes sparkled with laughter. She held out a small box wrapped in pink tissue paper.

"Hey, Heidi!" Zack was relieved to see his girlfriend. He smiled and stepped out on the porch. When they hugged, her hair brushed his face and he caught the scent of vanilla. Heidi's hair always smelled sweet.

Heidi pulled back a little and looked up at Zack. "Are you ready to go? I just want to give this present to Shellie before we leave."

Zack's smile disappeared. "I can't go out," he said. "My mom needs me to stay and help her with the party."

Heidi's face fell. "Oh. Why?"

Zack paused. *Why do I always have to explain where my dad is? I wish he would just stay home once in a while.* "Um, my dad had to work today."

"He did? On Shellie's birthday?" Heidi said in surprise. She sat down on the steps that led down from the porch to the walkway.

"Yeah, well, he's been putting in a *lot* of overtime lately. My mom is pretty mad at him," Zack said, sitting down beside her. He tried to make it sound like it wasn't a big deal, even thought he knew it was. His dad was spending all his time at the office. He even ate dinner there. Which meant that his parents were fighting more than ever. Zack hated talking about it. He *really* hated talking about it to Heidi. Her family was so normal. No one ever argued at her house. His own parents seemed to argue every time they were in the same room.

Heidi opened her mouth to say something. She was interrupted by a loud SPLAT! A water balloon landed on the step in front of them and soaked their feet. Zack looked up and saw two faces looking down over the window ledge.

"Good one, Patrick!" said Zack's younger brother, Michael. He gave his friend a high-five. Then he fired another water balloon at Zack.

The balloon was way off. Zack didn't even move as it landed on the brick path leading away from the steps. He glared up at the boys. "You're dead meat when you come down here, Michael!" Zack shouted. The only reply was a howl of laughter from above.

"Stupid jerks," Zack muttered, scowling up at the window. "Why do they act like a couple of little kids?"

Heidi tried not to laugh. "I guess he learned from the best, right Zack?" she said. She stretched out her legs to dry in the sun.

"What? You mean *me*?" he asked, frowning a little. Then a smile crept over his face. "Well, maybe I did throw a few water balloons when I was a kid," he admitted. "But I quit acting like that *way* before *I* was fourteen."

Suddenly, the sound of shrieking came from the backyard. "Uh oh, do you think Michael is crashing the party? Or should I say *splashing* the party?" Heidi joked.

Zack stood up. "Who knows? My mom is probably going nuts. Let's go see if the food is ready yet," he said.

The first thing Zack saw in the backyard was a clown. He was wearing a bright orange wig topped with a shiny, round black hat. On top of the hat sat a tiny toy mouse. It was also wearing a tiny, shiny hat. The clown's pants were covered with wild stripes in rainbow colors. He wore a bright red shirt with a huge yellow bow tie. His face was painted white, with a wide red mouth and rosy cheeks.

A crowd of little kids had gathered around the clown. He was twisting balloons and making animal shapes. Zack's mom stood off to one side, grilling hamburgers and hot dogs. Michael was nowhere in sight.

Shellie zoomed over to Zack and Heidi. Her blue eyes were wide with excitement. "Guess what, Zack! Mom got a clown for the party! His name is Bobo, and he does magic tricks!"

"That's awesome, Shel," Zack said with a grin. He watched her run back to join her group of friends clustered around Bobo. For a moment, he thought of his own sixth birthday. He remembered going to the water park. His parents had taken him with Michael and a group of boys. Shellie hadn't even been born then. He remembered his dad wheeling a new blue bike out of the garage. It had been a pretty cool birthday.

Zack watched Shellie giggling with her friends. He felt a surge of anger toward his dad. *He should be here*, he thought. *Parents aren't supposed to miss your birthday.*

"Hey, Earth to Zack!" Heidi teased. "What are you thinking about? You look kind of mad."

Zack didn't feel like explaining it to Heidi. It was just the same old thing. His dad wasn't around. His mom was mad. And now he was stuck at his little sister's birthday party. "Nothing," he said, shrugging it off.

"Let's get a hamburger. I'm starving." Heidi pulled him over to the barbecue.

"Hi, kids! Who's brave enough to try a burger?" Mrs. Brown asked. She waved one hand at the grill. "They're kind of...well done."

Barbecuing was always Mr. Brown's job. The burgers were pretty burnt. Zack made a face.

"Um…I guess I'll have one, Mom," he said with a sideways glance at Heidi.

"Me too, Mrs. Brown," Heidi said. If she was grossed out, she didn't show it. That was Heidi. She was so easygoing. Not like Zack. He took everything so seriously. Like the time they stood in line to get tickets to see the Rolling Stones. They had waited all night, but the tickets sold out just before they got to the booth. Zack had complained about it for weeks. In fact, it still bugged him.

"Another weekend ruined by Dad," Zack said under his breath. He knew his mother could probably hear him, but he didn't care. He was mad at her, too. *Why do I always have to suffer when Dad skips out?* he thought. *It's not my fault he's never here. I shouldn't have to waste my weekend hanging around with a bunch of little kids. Mom never makes Michael help out.*

His mother stopped smiling. She slapped a burger onto Zack's plate. "I'm sorry your day is ruined, Zack," she said between gritted teeth. "But your sister isn't even going to have a birthday cake today. All I'm asking for is a little help. Do you think you can manage that?" She put her hands on her hips and stared him down.

Zack frowned and looked at the ground. He was aware of Heidi standing just behind him. He felt his face burning with anger and frustration. "Fine," he snapped. He turned and started walking away.

"Excuse me?" said Mrs. Brown, raising her eyebrows at him.

Zack sighed heavily. He turned around. "Yes, Mom. I'll stay and help," he said, forcing himself to sound polite.

"Thank you." Mrs. Brown turned back to the food, which was turning black and crusty on the grill.

chapter 3

ta-da!

Zack and Heidi went to sit at a table under a tall birch tree. Heidi didn't say a word about Zack's grumpy mood. He was still scowling in anger. Every weekend it was the same story. His dad wasn't around, so Zack had to stay home and do extra chores. Last weekend, he and his best friend, Leo Spinelli, had planned to go biking. But Zack's mom had to go out. She needed someone to stay home with Shellie. Michael had already left with his friends so Zack got stuck at home. Again.

Zack piled pickles and ketchup on his burger and took a huge bite. He glanced over at Bobo the clown, who was pulling long silk scarves out of his sleeve. The kids clapped and cheered loudly.

"Watch this, kids! For my next trick, I'm going to make this hot dog disappear!" Bobo held a paper plate in the air and gestured dramatically. "One…two…three!"

Zack watched as Bobo lifted the hot dog off the plate. Then he stuffed it in his mouth, chewing rapidly. His cheeks bulged.

"Ta-daaaa!" said Bobo in a muffled voice. Bits of hot dog flew out of his big red mouth.

The kids stared at him, looking cheated. "That was a dumb trick," said Shellie, glaring up at Bobo. She spun around and grinned at her friends. "Let's open my presents!" she said.

"Yaaaaaaayyyyyy!" yelled her friends. They all ran toward the house.

Zack shook his head and snorted. "I think my mom should get her money back for that clown," he said. "He *sucks*." He watched as Bobo walked toward the picnic table.

"Here he comes," Heidi said.

Zack stared as Bobo sat down. The clown dug into the bowl of potato chips on the table. There was something so familiar about him.

He looked closely at Bobo. Zack could see the guy's real hair sticking out under his wig. Bleached blond. A small gold earring dangled from one ear. Just like…

"Leo?" said Zack in disbelief.

The clown stopped eating. He turned slowly to face Zack and Heidi. "Ah...I'm busted," said the clown with a wide grin. He pulled off his wig and hat.

Zack burst out laughing. It was his best friend, Leo. He hadn't recognized him in that silly clown outfit. Normally, Leo wore baggy pants and T-shirts. His blond hair was always uncombed and messy. Bowler hats and bow ties were not exactly his style.

"Dude, I didn't recognize you with that wig!" said Zack, gasping with laughter.

Leo's face would have turned red if he hadn't been wearing so much makeup. "Yeah, well, nobody else needs to know about this," he said in a warning tone of voice. "Okay?"

Heidi was trying not to choke on her hamburger. "Leo, what are you *doing?*" she asked, giggling.

"I'm making money. What else?" said Leo with a shrug. "Hey, it beats making donuts at Donut Man," he teased. Heidi made a face and threw a potato chip at him. He grabbed it and tossed it in his mouth, grinning his red-and-white clown smile at her.

It turned out Leo had found the job listed in the newspaper. "I needed a job. I'm saving up for a car," he explained.

Zack snorted. "You'll have to make a lot more balloon animals to save that much money," he said.

"It pays pretty good," Leo shot back. "Hey, Zack, make sure your mom gives me a nice tip," he added.

"I think you're eating your tip right now," Zack said.

Leo wolfed down a handful of chips. He finished gulping down a can of soda and wiped his mouth. "I'm going home to wash this stuff off my face," he said, standing up. He pretended to straighten his plastic bow tie. Then he smoothed the wrinkles out of his enormous pants. "Later, dudes!" he called over his shoulder.

Heidi shook her head. "What a goof. He's the perfect clown. Well, except for the hot dog trick," she remarked with a grin.

"Yeah," Zack agreed. He leaned back against the picnic table and stretched his arms over his head.

Heidi stood up. She started to clean up the mess on the picnic table. Zack put out his hand to stop her. "Heidi, you don't have to do that," he said. "I'll do it."

"It's okay," said Heidi. "I don't mind. You guys can use the help today, right?" She smiled up at Zack. He could tell she was trying to be really nice. She knew he was in a bad mood, but it just made him feel worse. He didn't want her to feel sorry for him.

She must think my parents are so weird, he thought. Heidi's parents always seemed happy. Neither of them skipped out of dinner on a regular basis, like his dad did. When school finished in three weeks, Heidi was going on a family holiday. In the two months they had been dating, Zack had never heard her parents arguing like his did.

His parents never used to argue so much. Things were fine before his dad started working so much overtime. Now it seemed like they fought all the time. Sometimes they argued right in front of Zack, Michael, and Shellie. Most of the time Zack overheard his parents fighting at night. Their voices carried through the heating duct between his bedroom and their room. Those fights were way worse. They didn't think anyone could hear them, and they said some pretty nasty things to each other. Those times, Zack just put on his headphones or played his guitar to drown them out.

Out of the corner of his eye, Zack saw his mother waving him over. He groaned.

"My mom wants me for something," he said. "I'd better go and see what she wants."

Zack's mother handed him the tray of cupcakes. "Can you pass these out, please?" she asked. "I've got one with a candle ready for Shellie." She didn't smile or thank him. She just turned around and walked away.

Zack took the tray. He watched his mom light the candle on his sister's cupcake. All of Shellie's friends began to sing "Happy Birthday." *Some happy birthday this is*, Zack thought sourly.

chapter 4

over the edge

In spite of Zack's bad mood, the rest of the afternoon passed quickly. Soon it was time to hand out goody bags to all the sticky little party guests. The yard began to clear out as people left. After the last person was gone, Zack threw himself into in a chair on the deck.

Heidi walked over to stand in front of him. She put her hands on his shoulders and leaned down so that their faces were almost touching. "Do you want me to stay and help clean up?" she asked.

Zack shook his head. "No, it's okay. We can handle it," he said. He could tell his mother was in a bad mood. *When Dad gets home, it's going to be World War Three,* he thought. He really didn't want Heidi to see it.

"Okay," said Heidi. She leaned forward and kissed him.

"*Ewwwwww!* Mom! Zack's kissing Heidi!" yelled a shrill voice behind them. Zack swiveled around to see Shellie standing there.

Heidi laughed. Zack stood up straight. He glared at his little sister. It was enough to send her shrieking up the steps of the deck. Zack took Heidi's hand. He walked her out to the driveway and they finished saying good-bye.

Zack went back to help his mom clean up the backyard. "Hey, Mom, where's Michael?" Zack realized that he hadn't seen his younger brother all afternoon.

"He went to Patrick's house. You know how he terrorizes Shellie and her friends. I thought it would just be easier if I sent him out for the day," said Mrs. Brown. She picked up a tray loaded with leftover food. She walked carefully toward the house. Zack thought she looked tired. She seemed a lot older all of a sudden.

Mrs. Brown had always been one of the busiest parents Zack knew. She was an accountant. After Shellie was born, she decided to work part-time. She drove Michael and Shellie to all their sports practices and music lessons. She was the head of the parent committee at Shellie's school. On top of all her other jobs, she cooked most of the meals, did the laundry, and kept the house clean. Mr. Brown always seemed to get out of his chores because he was busy working. Which meant that Zack got stuck doing a lot of them.

Zack frowned as he thought of his dad. He checked his watch. It was almost five-thirty.

"When is Dad coming home?" Zack asked his mother. He tossed a bag of trash into the bin behind the garage.

"I don't know," Mrs. Brown said. She balanced the tray on one arm and tried to open the back door. The tray wobbled and she nearly dropped it.

"Here, Mom, I'll do it," Zack said, grabbing the door. He followed her into the house.

A red light flashed on the phone. Mrs. Brown set down the tray and walked over to check the messages. Zack washed his hands at the kitchen sink and watched his mom out of the corner of his eye. Her frown deepened as she listened to the message. Then she gasped and hung up the phone.

"Who was it?" Zack asked quickly. He wondered if something had happened to his dad. *Maybe that's why he's so late,* he thought. His pulse quickened. He felt a little guilty for thinking badly of his dad a moment ago.

Mrs. Brown grabbed her keys and purse. "That was Patrick's father. Michael has been taken to the hospital. I don't know what happened exactly. Mr. Neilson said something about Michael falling off something. I'll call you when I find out." She yanked open the door. "Stay here with Shellie!" she called over her shoulder as she ran out.

chapter 5

a bad break

She never called. It was past eight o'clock when Zack heard a key turn in the lock. He leaped from the sofa and ran to the door. Shellie followed close behind him.

Zack's father stood in the hallway, smiling at Shellie and Zack. Shellie shouted, "Daddeeee!" She launched herself into his arms.

"Oof!" Mr. Brown dropped his briefcase and caught her just in time. "How's my big girl?" he asked, hugging her tightly.

Shellie pulled back and looked up at him. "You didn't come to my birthday party, Dad," she said with a frown.

A guilty look crossed Mr. Brown's handsome face. "I know, honey. I'm sorry. I had to work today." He looked at Zack. "Hey, buddy—"

Zack cut him off. "Mom had to go to the hospital. Michael got hurt today."

Mr. Brown looked alarmed. "What happened? He's at the hospital? Is he all right?"

Zack shrugged. "I don't know."

"Well, what did your mother say?"

"She hasn't called us yet," said Zack.

"Okay, then let's go to the hospital," his dad said. "Shellie, get your shoes on." Shellie ran down the hall to get her shoes and jacket. Zack and his father stood alone in the hallway.

They were silent for a moment. Then Mr. Brown said, "How was the birthday party?"

"Like you care," Zack snapped. He knew he was being rude, but he didn't care. His dad should have been around to help his mom. Then maybe his mom wouldn't have sent Michael over to Patrick's house. *None of this would have happened,* he thought angrily.

Mr. Brown opened his mouth to say something. He stopped as headlights lit up the driveway. A car pulled in, and the engine stopped. "That must be your mom," he said. He turned and went outside.

A few minutes later, Mr. Brown stepped in the door. He was supporting Michael on one arm. Michael's face was pale. His left arm was covered in a plaster cast. Mrs. Brown came in behind them. She looked tense and tired. Zack followed them down the hall to the kitchen.

"There you go, Mike," Mr. Brown said, gently easing Michael into a chair.

Mrs. Brown tossed her purse on the table. "Sorry we were gone so long. The doctor had to wait for the X-rays to come back. We had to stop at the pharmacy and pick up some painkillers," she said. She patted Zack on the arm as she passed by him.

"What happened?" Mr. Brown asked.

"I fell off Patrick's garage," Michael said. He looked down at the floor.

"What! How?" his father asked.

Michael sighed and glanced up at his mother. She was leaning against the counter with her arms crossed over her chest. She simply raised her eyebrows. Clearly, she had already heard the story.

Michael cleared his throat. "Well, Patrick and I were kicking a soccer ball around his backyard. We could hear a bunch of girls next door. They've got a pool," he explained.

"Go on," Mr. Brown said.

Michael looked quickly at his mother again. He said, "Well...we decided to try and see over the fence. To see what...uh...what the girls were doing." His face was starting to turn red.

"Yes…?" Mr. Brown said.

"We thought we could see better if we went up on the garage roof. So we put a ladder up against the back of the garage. After we got up there, we could see everything," Michael said. He started to grin but stopped when he saw the grim look on his father's face.

"But Alicia saw us," Michael continued. "She's in our class at school. She started yelling and her dad came out of the house, and we tried to get down. I guess I lost my balance, and then I fell off the roof." He avoided his dad's stare.

Mr. Brown cleared his throat. Zack was pretty sure his dad was trying not to laugh. "Well, I'm glad you're not seriously hurt. But that was a dangerous thing to do. You must have fallen at least ten or twelve feet, Michael. You could have broken your neck."

"I know, Dad," Michael muttered. "I'm sorry, okay?"

Mr. Brown nodded. "All right. I guess there's no point grounding you. You're going to be in that cast for six weeks anyway. You'd better get up to bed and try to go to sleep now. Those painkillers should kick in pretty soon. "

"And you too, birthday girl," Mrs. Brown said, taking Shellie's hand. "It's eight-thirty. Time for bed."

"Aw, Mom, I don't *want* to go to bed," said Shellie. Her face split in a huge yawn and she blinked sleepily as her mother led her down the hall toward the stairs.

Michael got painfully to his feet. "'Night," he said.

"I'll help you, Mike," Zack said quickly. He didn't want to stay in the kitchen alone with his dad. He was still mad at him.

chapter 6

Brown vs. Brown,
round one

Zack and Michael shared a bedroom on the second floor. The walls were covered with posters. Dirty socks, comic books, and soccer cleats littered the floor on Michael's side. Michael kicked a soccer ball out of his way and sat on the edge of his bed.

"Do you...ah...want a hand getting your pajamas on?" Zack asked.

Michael shook his head. "No, I can do it," he said. He managed to unzip his jeans with one hand and let them drop to the floor.

Zack was putting away his guitar. He turned around and saw Michael struggling to get his T-shirt off. "Here, I'll do it, Mike," Zack said, going over to help his younger brother.

"No! I can—"

"No, you can't. Just sit still," said Zack. Michael stopped resisting and sat still while Zack helped him out of his shirt.

"So?" Zack raised his eyebrows at his brother.

"So what?" Michael said with a blank look.

"Was it worth it?" asked Zack.

"Worth it?" Michael looked confused. Then he realized what Zack meant. "Oh…yeah, it was totally worth it," he said with a grin. "Alicia Anderson looks great in a bikini."

Michael fell asleep right away. The painkillers knocked him out. Zack looked at the clock. *It's not even nine o'clock yet*, he thought. He wondered what was on TV.

Halfway down the stairs, Zack heard his parents' voices coming from the kitchen. He stopped, not sure whether to keep walking.

"…needed you today," his mother was saying. Her voice was low, but angry.

"Don't try to make me feel guilty, Denise. Someone has to work to pay the bills around here," Zack's father said.

"Oh, I suppose you think I don't work?" Mrs. Brown said, her voice rising. "Do you really believe that taking care of the house and the kids isn't work? And in case you've forgotten, I'm *still* putting in three days a week at the office. I work every day, Andrew. From seven in the morning until ten at night. I drive Shellie to piano. I take Michael to soccer practice. Plus I help them with their homework. I can't do it all by myself!"

"Look, I said I'm sorry I wasn't here today. I'll try to put in some time around the house this week, okay?" Mr. Brown said.

Zack heard his mother say angrily, "Andrew, this house is not a jail cell. Spending time with your family is not 'putting in time.' What is *wrong* with you lately?"

"There's nothing wrong with me," replied Mr. Brown in a tense voice. "The office is just busy right now. I need to be there."

"Well, we need you to be *here*. See if you can pencil us in sometime next week, okay?" Mrs. Brown shot back.

A chair scraped across the kitchen floor. Zack heard footsteps coming toward him. He didn't know whether it was his mom or his dad, but he didn't want to find out. Quickly, he turned around and tiptoed back upstairs.

Zack switched on the lamp next to his bed. He glanced over at Michael, who was still asleep. He was lying on his back with his broken arm supported by a pillow. His mouth was open, and he wheezed a little in his sleep. He didn't move, even when Zack turned on the light.

Zack threw himself down on his bed. He lay on his back and stared at the ceiling. *Why do they always have to fight? I'm sick of listening to them every night.*

It was still way too early to go to sleep. *What am I supposed to do now?* he thought. *I can't play my guitar—that would wake up Michael for sure. I could call Heidi,* he thought. *She's probably home.* The phone was in the kitchen, though. No way was he going downstairs.

He put on his headphones and grabbed a music magazine off the floor. The music helped take his mind off things.

chapter 7

breakfast at
the Browns'

Zack woke up the next morning to the sound of his mother's voice. She was standing in his bedroom, dressed for work. She walked over to the window and threw open the curtains. Bright sunlight flooded the room.

"All right, boys, time to get up!" Mrs. Brown said loudly. She went to Michael's bed and bent over him. "Michael, how does your arm feel?"

"Hurts," Michael grunted. He struggled to sit up. "Have to take a wizz," he mumbled.

"Here, let me help you—"

"*Mom!* I don't want you to help me in the bathroom!" Michael said in a horrified voice. "I can do it myself!"

His mother gave a sigh. "I wasn't going to come in the bathroom with you. I'm just trying to help you get out of bed. You're going to be late for school if you don't hurry."

She smiled at Zack. "Zack, help your brother get ready for school, please. I have to finish making lunch for Michael and Shellie." She turned and went out.

"Go and use the bathroom," Zack said to Michael, yawning widely. "Call me if you need some help with your clothes."

"Yeah, whatever," Michael grumbled.

Twenty minutes later, they thumped down the stairs and into the kitchen. Shellie was already sitting at the table. Her blond curls were pulled into two tight pigtails on either side of her head. "Good morning, Mike," she said.

"Morning."

"Does your arm hurt?" Shellie asked. She looked curiously at his cast.

"Yes."

"How come you were spying on Patrick's neighbor?" she asked.

"That's none of your business," Michael muttered. He bent closer to his cereal bowl and did his best to ignore her.

"But I want to know."

"So what?"

"Mom, why won't Michael tell me why he was spying?" Shellie asked.

"Because Michael's arm hurts, and he isn't feeling well," Mrs. Brown replied. "Do you want a banana, Shellie?"

Shellie made a face. "I don't like bananas."

Mrs. Brown gave her a stern look. "You liked them last week."

"Well, I don't like them anymore," Shellie said. She turned back to her cereal. The list of foods Shellie didn't like was getting longer by the day. She was a very picky eater.

"Zack? Banana?" His mother waved the fruit at him.

"Sure," Zack said. He took it and sat down at the table. He reached for a piece of toast and began spreading peanut butter on it. As he chewed, he noticed that his father wasn't sitting at the table yet.

"Where's Dad?" he asked with his mouth full of peanut butter.

"He went to the office early today," Mrs. Brown answered. Her face looked really tight and tense. Zack decided not to ask any more questions about his dad. He finished his toast and went upstairs. He grabbed his car keys, made sure he had money for lunch, and ran back downstairs.

"I'm leaving now," he said, poking his head into the kitchen.

"Wait up," said Michael. He drained the milk from his cereal bowl and stood up.

"Don't forget your lunch," his mother said.

"Oh, yeah, thanks," said Michael. He grabbed his lunch bag off the counter and followed Zack outside.

Mrs. Brown's old blue car was parked in the driveway. She stopped driving it after she got a new minivan the year before. It wasn't a great-looking car, but it was still in pretty good shape. Zack was the only one who drove it now. Michael was always begging him for a ride. Zack agreed to drive him to school. There was no way he was going to drive Michael all over town, though.

It was a short drive to Bayview High from the Brown house. Michael and Zack went their own ways as soon as they got out of the car.

Zack walked upstairs to his locker. His first class was math with Mr. O'Grady. It was his best subject. He was turning a corner on the third floor when he heard a voice call out, "Zack! Wait up!" He looked back over his shoulder. Leo was running toward him.

"Dude! I've been trying to catch you since first floor," Leo said. After chasing Zack up two flights of stairs, Leo wasn't even breathing hard. He had played soccer for years. He was in great shape. Leo didn't have Zack's wide shoulders and he weighed a good twenty pounds less than Zack. He was lean but not skinny. He was tougher than he looked, too.

"What's up?" said Zack, tossing his backpack into his locker.

"I need to borrow your notes from Spanish. Cortes is giving a quiz today, and I missed the last class. I'm going to study on my free period this morning," Leo explained. He looked around, just in case Señora Cortes was nearby.

"Sure," Zack said. He pulled a binder from his locker. He removed some notes and handed them to Leo.

"Thanks, man," Leo said. He stuffed the notes into his backpack. "I owe you one."

"No problem." Zack shut his locker. He looked over Leo's shoulder. A pretty girl with dark chestnut hair was walking toward them. She smiled when she saw Zack.

"Here comes your sister, Leo," he said.

Leo rolled his eyes. "Jodi, why do you have to follow me around?" he asked as she stopped in front of them.

"Hey, Zack, how's it going?" asked Jodi, ignoring Leo. "Great game last week. Too bad Bobo here wasn't on his game." She threw a dirty look at Leo.

"Shut up, Jodi," Leo snarled.

"I might try out for the girls' team next year." Jodi kept on talking as if Leo hadn't spoken. "Maybe you could show me some of your moves?" She smiled up at Zack, her dark eyes shining.

"Sure," Zack replied. Leo's face was turning the color of a ripe tomato.

"Great! See you later," Jodi said. She flipped back her long hair and walked off.

"Was she *flirting* with you?" Leo said, more to himself than to Zack as they walked toward math class.

Zack laughed. "No way! Jodi just thinks of me as a big brother. Anyway, I didn't know she was interested in soccer."

"I don't think that's all she's interested in," Leo said with a scowl.

chapter 8

learning curves

When Zack and Leo got to math class, Mr. O'Grady hadn't arrived yet. All the students were talking and laughing. They didn't notice a tall, slim, blond woman enter the room.

"Ahem!" she said loudly. She stood beside Mr. O'Grady's desk and waited for the class to quiet down. When everyone stopped talking, she smiled. "Hello, class. I'm Ms. Spencer. I'm filling in for Mr. O'Grady this week."

"A supply teacher! All *right!*" Leo whispered.

Zack nodded, but he was staring at Ms. Spencer. She looked about twenty-five years old. Her blond hair fell down past her shoulders in loose waves. *She's a teacher?* he thought.

"She's a lot better-looking than O'Grady," Zack said in a low voice.

A girl with a long ponytail and glasses put up her hand. "Is Mr. O'Grady sick?" she asked.

Ms. Spencer glanced at the seating chart posted on the blackboard. "You must be Elizabeth Gordon," she said. The girl nodded.

"Mr. O'Grady is at a conference this week," said Ms. Spencer. "He'll be back next Monday. Now, class, please turn to page eighty-three of your textbook. We'll keep working on recursive formulas…"

At the end of class, Zack and Leo packed up their books. They couldn't help checking out the pretty supply teacher one more time on their way out.

"Too bad Señora Cortes doesn't have legs like Ms. Spencer. I'd never miss class," Leo said.

Zack nodded. "Yeah, I know what you mean. Did you see her—"

"Her what?" asked a female voice.

Zack whipped around. Heidi stood just behind him, carrying an armload of books.

"Uh—nothing," Zack said quickly. He felt his face getting warm, and he tried to look casual. He didn't want Heidi to think he was checking out teachers. "We were just talking about…Spanish. Leo's Spanish quiz. He needs my notes."

"Got 'em already, dude," Leo said.

"Right," said Zack. "Good. Well, I'm going to be late for gym class. I'd better run."

Heidi gave him a strange look. "Yeah. See you later."

Why should I feel guilty? Zack thought as he ran down the stairs to the gym. *What's the big deal? So what if Ms. Spencer is pretty? She's a teacher. It's not like I'm going to ask her out or anything.*

After school that day, Zack went out to the parking lot. He found Michael waiting for him as usual. He was leaning against their car and talking to a dark-haired girl. As Zack walked closer, he saw that it was Leo's little sister, Jodi.

Jodi was not really "little." She was only a year younger than Leo and Zack. When she was twelve and the boys were thirteen, they had not paid any attention to her. She had always been an odd-looking kid. She was all skinny arms and legs, stringy hair, and a mouth full of braces.

But now that Jodi was sixteen, she wasn't so easy to ignore. Zack watched her talking to Michael. *She's really cute now,* he thought. She had really grown up over the past couple of years. Thanks to the braces, she had an amazing smile. And the boys at school noticed. It drove Leo nuts. He complained about it constantly. Zack just laughed at Leo. He kept telling Leo that he was way too protective. "Oh, yeah? Just wait until Shellie starts going out with guys," Leo kept saying. "You'll see what it's like when the whole soccer team is calling your house to talk to your *sister!*"

Zack walked up to Michael and Jodi just in time to hear Jodi say, "That's *awful*, Mike!"

"What's awful?" Zack asked.

Michael jumped. "Zack! I didn't see you there." His eyes darted to Jodi and back to Zack.

Jodi turned to smile at Zack. "You didn't tell me that Mike broke his arm playing soccer. I hope the guy who hit him got a suspension!"

"Oh. Right," said Zack with a faint grin. He looked at Michael out of the corner of his eye. "Playing soccer, huh?"

Michael looked like he was going to wet his pants. He shifted nervously from one foot to the other. "Yeah," he said in a choked voice.

Zack wasn't going to blow Michael's story. His little brother just wanted Jodi to think he was cool. He couldn't tell her that he was spying on the girls next door from Mr. Campbell's garage roof. "Yeah, it was a tough team," Zack said with a straight face. "Mike was lucky he didn't break his neck. He took a really bad fall."

Jodi shook her head in sympathy. "That's too bad, Mike. I hope you won't have to miss the dance next Friday."

"What dance?" asked Zack.

In answer, Jodi handed him a flyer from the stack she was carrying. "'Get your groove on at the Bayview High Retro Party,'" read Zack out loud. "'Tickets are five dollars from any student council representative—'"

"Like me," Jodi interrupted.

"'—and all proceeds will be donated to the Port Catherine soup kitchen.' Sounds like fun," said Zack.

"Yeah, it's going to be a blast," Jodi agreed. "We're having a retro theme. The music is going to be old stuff—well, mostly, but we'll have some new music, too. Everybody has to come dressed in retro clothes or else they have to pay an extra two dollars at the door. We're giving away prizes for the best costumes, too."

"Cool," said Michael.

"I hope you guys can come," Jodi said. "I have to go and put up these flyers. See you later!" She flashed a smile at Zack and left.

Michael seemed to be frozen to the spot as he watched Jodi walk back to the school. "Come on, Mike. Put your eyes back in your head and get in the car," Zack teased.

Michael glared at him and walked around to the passenger side. He eased himself into the car, being careful not to bump his arm.

"You told Jodi that you broke your arm playing soccer?" Zack said, trying not to laugh.

"Yes," Michael shot back.

"And she believed that?"

"Yes," said Michael. He was silent for a minute. Then he said, "Anyway, it doesn't matter what Jodi thinks of me...she likes *you*."

"As if!" Zack said with a laugh. "She's Leo's little sister, Mike! I've known her since she was five years old."

"Yeah, well, she definitely has a crush on you," said Michael. "I can totally see it when she looks at you."

Zack just shook his head. But he couldn't help wondering if Michael was right about Jodi. Sometimes he could tell that she was looking at him. And sometimes the looks were a little more than just friendly.

chapter 9

sucker punch

At home, the living room was empty and so was the kitchen. *That's weird. Mom is usually home by now. She must have gone out with Shellie,* Zack thought. His stomach rumbled. He went to the fridge, opened the door, and looked inside for a snack. *Cold pizza. Perfect,* he thought. He grabbed a soda and went to watch some TV.

By six o'clock, Zack was thinking about getting another snack. Just then, his mother's minivan pulled into the driveway. Zack looked out the window. He saw his mom walking up the driveway with Shellie.

"Hi, Mom," Zack said as they came in the door. "Where were you? We're starving."

Mrs. Brown didn't answer right away. She hung up her jacket and then knelt down in front of Shellie. His little sister was sitting on the bench near the front door. She was holding a hand over one ear. Her face was screwed up in pain and she looked like she had been crying.

Zack stood up and went over. "Hey, what's the matter, Shel?" he asked.

"My ear hurts," Shellie whimpered.

"She has an ear infection. I had to take her to the hospital to get medicine. We had to wait for the doctor for over an *hour*," said Mrs. Brown. "Boys, can you please order a pizza for supper? I didn't have time to pick up groceries." She pulled some money from her purse.

"Sure. What do you want on your pizza, Shellie? Lizard lips and frog fingers? Snail snot?" Michael teased. But Shellie just made a face and turned away.

"Leave her alone, Michael," his mother said gently. "She's got a fever. I'm going to put her to bed." She led Shellie toward the stairs. Halfway up, she stopped and called down to Zack, "Has your father phoned?"

"No," Zack said.

His mother's face hardened. "All right." She turned around and kept going up the stairs.

Mrs. Brown was upstairs for a long time. The pizza arrived just as she came down. Michael and Zack were loading their plates in the kitchen. Zack looked up as his mother came in. She was still dressed in the suit she had worn to work that day. She looked exhausted. She took a slice of pizza and sat down at the kitchen table. She just stared at it for a long time.

"Mom, you had better eat that," said Zack.

"I'll eat it if you don't want it," Michael offered. He pretended to make a grab for it.

Their mother grinned weakly. "Okay, okay." She picked at her pizza a little longer, and then she pushed it aside. She kept looking at the clock.

After dinner, they went to the living room to watch TV. Once or twice Mrs. Brown went upstairs to check on Shellie. During one checkup, Michael said to Zack, "Where's Dad?"

"I don't know," Zack replied. He had been wondering the same thing. It was getting late and his dad still wasn't home.

"Do you think Mom knows where he is?" asked Michael.

"I don't know."

They were quiet for a moment. Then Michael said, "They fight a lot. They never used to do that."

"Yeah, I know," Zack muttered. He didn't want to talk about it. He stared ahead at the TV and flicked to another channel.

"Zack, do you think—" Michael began.

"Look, Mike, I don't want to talk about Mom and Dad. Okay?" Zack hissed.

Michael glared back at him. "Fine. Whatever." He slumped farther down on the sofa and stared angrily at the TV.

Mrs. Brown came downstairs a few minutes later, yawning. "Michael, did you take your painkiller when you got home from school?"

"Yes," Michael answered. He dragged himself off the sofa, being careful not to lean on his bad arm. "I'm going to bed now."

Zack stretched out his legs and kept looking at the screen. He didn't want to look at his mom. Every time he looked at her, he saw how tired and worried and angry she was.

"I'm going to bed, too," Zack said abruptly, standing up. "Good night, Mom."

"'Night, honey," Mrs. Brown said from her chair. She hardly looked up at him.

A while later, Zack woke up suddenly. He looked around his darkened bedroom. The numbers on his alarm clock glowed red in the darkness. It was twenty minutes past midnight. Zack looked over at Michael. He was lying on his back, breathing deeply.

Zack slid out of bed and walked down the hall to the bathroom. When he came out, he noticed a light shining downstairs. The stairs led down to the front hallway. He peered over the banister, but he couldn't see anyone.

Zack turned back toward his room. Then he heard his father's voice say, "I'm sick and tired of arguing about this, Denise!"

Zack stopped. His neck prickled with alarm. He crept to the top of the stairs and leaned against the railing, listening.

His mother's voice floated upstairs. "This is the second time in a week that we needed you and you weren't here. You were supposed to pick up Shellie from the sitter! I had to leave work early, and *then* I had to take her to the hospital, and—"

"That wasn't my fault, Denise," interrupted Mr. Brown.

Mrs. Brown made a frustrated noise. "It wasn't your fault she had to go to the hospital. But you forgot to pick her up *again!*"

"I told you, I didn't *forget.* I had to stay late at the office," Mr. Brown argued.

Zack knew he shouldn't be listening to this, but he was frozen to the spot. His whole body seemed to be straining to hear.

"Every night the kids ask me where you are. I don't have any answers for them. What kind of father forgets to pick up his kids?" Mrs. Brown said angrily.

"So now I'm not a good father? Is that what you're trying to say?" Mr. Brown asked, his voice rising.

"No, but…I…I don't know!" Mrs. Brown said in frustration. "All I know is, you've changed. And I'm not happy anymore."

"Well, that makes two of us," Mr. Brown said coldly.

There was a scraping sound as a chair was pushed across the kitchen floor. Zack heard footsteps coming down the hallway to the front door. He stepped back into the shadows at the top of the stairs so he wouldn't be seen.

The light from the front hall shone down on Zack's parents. He could see his father's face. His dad looked furious. His mother stood a few feet away with her arms crossed over her chest. She looked like she was about to cry. Zack's stomach churned. He didn't want to hear anymore. It was too private and too painful. He turned around to go back to bed.

And then he heard his father say, "Denise, it's over. I want a divorce."

chapter 10

the sound of a heart breaking

Zack felt like he had been punched in the stomach. *Did I hear that right?* he thought. He looked down at his parents. They were standing at the front door and staring at each other.

Time seemed to stop for several minutes. Zack heard his mother say in a trembling voice, "You can't...you can't be serious."

Mr. Brown's face looked cold and hard under the hallway light. "I think it's best if I leave now. I will come back for my things sometime this week."

Zack watched his father open the front door. It felt like he was watching something happening in a movie. It couldn't be real. Without meaning to, he took a step forward. The floorboard creaked slightly.

His father's eyes flicked upward. His gaze searched the shadows, but he didn't seem to see Zack standing there. Without another word, he turned around and walked out. The door clicked shut behind him. The house was totally silent after he was gone.

Down below, his mother was standing straight and still. Her hands were balled into fists at her sides. Her back was to Zack, so he couldn't see her face. Her body sagged, and she sat down on the bottom step. She leaned forward suddenly. For a moment Zack wondered if she was going to throw up.

Zack started to go downstairs, but he stopped when he heard his mother crying. He had only seen her cry once before. She had cried when his grandfather died six years ago. That was different, though. Her shoulders were shaking now. She was making an awful choking noise, as if she were trying to keep the sounds inside. Zack didn't know what to do.

Suddenly, his mother stood up. Zack stepped back into the dark hallway at the top of the stairs. Mrs. Brown walked slowly down the hall toward the kitchen. A moment later, Zack heard the back door open quietly and then close.

Zack went to the window at the end of the hall that looked out over the backyard. He could see his mom sitting in a wicker rocking chair on the deck. She wasn't moving. Even though Zack couldn't hear her, he could tell she was crying. Something told him it would be better to leave her alone for a while.

Zack crawled back into bed and lay staring up at the ceiling. Even though he had just watched his parents break up, his mind would not accept it. He kept replaying it in his mind, like a scene from a movie.

How could Dad leave like that? Zack thought. He knew his parents were having problems, but he hadn't seen that one coming. *Where is he going to sleep tonight, anyway? Is he just going to call up one of his friends and say, "Hey, I left my wife and kids. Mind if I stay in your spare bedroom?"*

Zack kicked off his blankets angrily. *What a jerk! Why is he doing this to us? What did we ever do to him?*

He tried not to think about it, but he could think of nothing else. It was almost dawn when he finally fell asleep.

The next morning Zack woke up before the alarm went off. He felt tired and restless, as though he had had bad dreams all night. He looked over at Michael. He was still sleeping. Zack felt his throat get tight as he thought about what he had seen and heard last night.

Maybe it really was just a bad dream, he thought. But he knew from the sick feeling in the pit of his stomach that it was real. He rolled onto one side and shut his eyes. He wondered what was going to happen next. *Will they sell the house? I think that's what happens when people get divorced. Then they go to court.*

An awful thought suddenly popped into his head. *Who's going to get custody of me and Mike and Shellie?* Zack was seventeen. He was old enough to decide where he wanted to live. He wondered if he would have to choose between his parents. Michael and Shellie wouldn't have a choice. Everybody knew kids who had divorced parents. They had to go back and forth between the parents' new houses. They spent one weekend with their mom and the next one with their dad.

Who decides all this stuff? he wondered. *A judge, probably.* He hoped with all his heart that he wouldn't have to pick one of his parents. He didn't think he could do it.

Zack knew that if he stayed in bed much longer the alarm would go off and wake up Michael. He really didn't want to be the one to tell his brother what had happened between their parents. He shut off the alarm and went down the hall to the bathroom.

After a quick shower, he got dressed for school and went downstairs. The house was deadly quiet. Zack walked into the kitchen. He wasn't sure what he was expecting to see. For some reason he was very nervous.

Normally, his mom would have been up for a few hours already. The coffeemaker would be dripping. The radio would be on. Breakfast would be on the table. Shellie's and Mike's lunches would be packed and ready to go.

This morning, the kitchen was empty. The blinds were closed and the room was dark and still. A mug sat on the table, half full of cold coffee. It was weird to find the kitchen so quiet on a Tuesday morning.

Where is everyone? Zack wondered. *They can't be sleeping.* He glanced up at the clock. It was almost eight o'clock. Confused, Zack walked into the living room, but it was empty too. *Why isn't anyone up yet?*

Now Zack was worried. His mother was *always* on time. She never slept late. Not even on weekends. This was a very bad sign. He ran upstairs and went to his parents' bedroom. The door was closed. He paused for a moment and then knocked softly. "Mom?" he called.

There was no answer. Zack knocked again, but she still didn't reply. He stood there for a moment, wondering what to do. *Should I wake her up?* He thought of his mother sitting in the backyard in the middle of night, crying. A lump formed in his throat.

She probably didn't sleep very much last night. Maybe I should just leave her alone, he thought. He backed away from the door and walked down the hall toward his bedroom.

Michael was still sleeping when Zack entered the room. He poked Michael's leg. "Hey, Mike," he said. Michael didn't stir. "Mike, wake up," Zack said a little louder. "Come on, we're going to be late for school."

Michael groaned. He opened his eyes slowly. He stared at Zack, who was standing at the foot of his bed.

"We're going to be late," Zack repeated. "Get dressed. I have to go wake up Shellie." He turned to go.

Michael sat up and rubbed his eyes. "Where's Mom?" he asked sleepily.

Zack paused. *I was hoping he wouldn't ask that*, he thought. *What am I supposed to say?* "She's sick," he said finally. "Don't wake her up, okay?"

After Zack woke Shellie, he went back downstairs. He began pulling out boxes of cereal. Michael and Shellie came into the kitchen, arguing loudly. Shellie's curly hair was sticking up all over her head.

"Cut it out, Michael," Shellie said. She gave him a push and went to sit at the table. Zack put a cereal bowl in front of her.

"My ear hurts," Shellie whined. "Where's Mom, Zack?"

"She's in bed. She doesn't feel well," Zack said. *Well, it's not exactly a lie*, he thought.

Michael slid into a chair and grabbed the box of Sugar Loops. He poured himself a bowl of cereal. "Where's Dad?" he asked through a mouthful of Sugar Loops.

The question took Zack by surprise. "He's… uh…he had to go to work early," he said.

"Oh," said Michael. He didn't seem surprised to hear that.

"Hurry up, guys. The bus will be here any minute," Zack said.

Shellie reached for the Sugar Loops. She started to fill her bowl, but the box was empty. "Hey, I wanted Sugar Loops," she said, frowning at Michael.

"Too bad," he mumbled through a mouthful of cereal.

Zack pushed a box of Fruity Flakes toward her. "Have some of this," he said.

"No. I want Sugar Loops," Shellie pouted.

"Well, there aren't any left," Zack said. He felt his temper rising again.

"Then I want toast," Shellie said. "With peanut butter, please."

Zack pushed back his chair with a sigh and got up to put bread in the toaster.

Michael chewed his cereal loudly. He poked Shellie in the arm. When she looked at him, he opened his mouth to show her the half-chewed cereal inside.

"Ugh! Stop it, Michael! Zack, Michael is being gross!" Shellie said, screwing up her face in disgust.

Zack looked up from spreading peanut butter on Shellie's toast. He glared at his younger brother. Michael promptly shut his mouth and pretended to look innocent. *This is crazy*, Zack thought as he put a plate of toast in front of Shellie. *Mom had better get up soon!*

chapter 11

playing mom

There was no time to wash the dishes so Zack stacked them in the sink. Michael went upstairs to brush his teeth. *Maybe I should check on Mom,* Zack thought, but Shellie tugged his sleeve.

"I need you to do my hair, Zack," she said. She handed him a hairbrush and a handful of rubber bands.

Zack stared at her. "You've got to be kidding, right?"

"Mom *always* does my hair. Just make two pigtails," Shellie said. She plunked down in a chair and waited.

"I don't believe this," Zack muttered. He held the brush over Shellie's head. He had no idea how to make pigtails. He started brushing her hair.

"Owww! That *hurts!*" she cried.

"Sorry!" Zack growled.

Just then Michael walked into the kitchen. He took one look at Zack and Shellie and burst out laughing.

"Hey, Zack, can you do mine next?" he asked in a high, girlish voice.

"Shut up, Michael," Zack warned. He tried to wind a rubber band around a handful of Shellie's curly hair. It popped off his finger and rolled away under the table.

Michael strolled over to the counter. "Where are our lunches?" he asked.

"What lunches?" Zack grunted. He struggled with another rubber band. It popped off his finger again and bounced onto the floor. "*Arrrggg!*" he groaned. "I can't *do* this!"

"Duh, our *lunches,*" Michael said, rolling his eyes. "You know, for school?"

Zack managed to make two pigtails in Shellie's hair. One was higher than the other one. Her part was a bit crooked, but it would have to do. "Okay, that's it, I'm done," Zack said to Shellie. "Go and get your school stuff." She hopped off the chair. Zack turned to Michael, who was waiting for an answer about lunch.

"Can't you make your own lunch?" Zack asked. "You're fourteen years old!"

Michael shook his head. "No, I don't have time. I have to take out the trash this morning."

"Okay, lunch…" Zack didn't know where to start. He hadn't taken a lunch to school since grade school. He always bought his lunch at Bayview. Their mom still packed a lunch for Michael every day.

Zack turned to his brother. "What does Mom usually put in your lunch?" he asked.

Michael shrugged. "Just some cookies, a bag of potato chips, and a chocolate bar. The usual."

Zack felt his temper rising. "Mike, you've got three seconds to tell me or I swear, you can go to school with no lunch at all."

"All right, all right," said Michael. "A tuna sandwich, an apple, and some cookies." He went outside.

Zack started slapping sandwiches together. It was almost twenty past eight. The bus would be coming to pick up Shellie at eight-thirty. Shellie came back into the kitchen. She was dragging her backpack behind her.

Zack gave Shellie her lunch box. She opened it and sniffed the contents.

"I don't like tuna," she said firmly.

"Of course you don't," Zack said between clenched teeth. He was barely holding onto his temper now. "What do you want instead?"

"I want peanut butter," Shellie said. "I don't like chocolate chip cookies, either."

"*What?* Who doesn't like chocolate chip cookies?" Zack shouted.

His sister's lower lip began to tremble. "Don't yell at me," she said with a frown.

Zack took a deep breath. "Sorry," he said. He remade Shellie's lunch as fast as possible.

They made it outside just in time to see the school bus rumbling away down the street.

"*Crap!*" Zack shouted.

"There goes the bus," Michael said, grinning. "Now what?"

Zack stomped up the driveway. "Let's go. I'll drive both of you."

Zack had to drive across town to drop off Shellie at school. He and Michael arrived at Bayview High ten minutes late for first class.

Michael stopped at the school doors and turned to Zack. "Wait! I forgot something," he said. "I need five bucks."

"What for?" Zack asked.

"I'm going on a class trip to the science center," Michael explained. "I need my permission form signed, too." He pulled a crumpled piece of paper from his pocket.

Zack stared at him. The day just kept getting worse. He grabbed the permission slip and wrote "Denise Brown" on it. He hoped Michael's science teacher wouldn't ask any questions. He dug in his jeans pocket for some money. All he had was a ten-dollar bill—his lunch money. With a sigh, he handed it over.

"Thanks!" Michael said with a grin. He took the money and ran up the stairs.

I'm never having kids, Zack thought as he trudged up the stairs. *They're way too much work.*

chapter 12

questions and answers

It was twenty past nine when Zack finally walked into math class. He was surprised to see Ms. Spencer standing at the blackboard. Then he remembered that she was teaching for Mr. O'Grady all week.

She turned and smiled at Zack when he came in the door. In spite of his bad mood, he grinned back. *She's way too pretty to be a teacher*, he thought as he took his seat in front of Leo.

Ms. Spencer looked at the seating plan and found Zack's name. A strange look crossed her face. She glanced at Zack.

"Zack Brown, correct?" she said.

"Yes. Sorry I'm late," he answered.

"That's all right. Open your book to page ninety-five," she said. She seemed to be watching him as he opened his math books. She didn't say anything else, though.

Zack could not focus on math. He kept thinking about his parents. *Maybe Dad will change his mind,* he thought. *He was mad, but he'll calm down. It was all just a big mistake. He wouldn't really divorce Mom.* Zack tried to convince himself it wasn't a big deal. Deep down, he knew things were pretty bad. His parents had been fighting for so long. Things just seemed to get worse and worse every time they argued.

Who's going to tell Mike and Shellie? he wondered. *I guess Mom will have to tell them tonight.* He still couldn't believe his mother had stayed in bed that morning.

When the bell rang loudly, Zack jumped in his seat. Class was over. He had not heard a word Ms. Spencer said.

"Hey, Zack, did you sleep in?" Leo asked as they grabbed their books and made their way out with the rest of the class.

"No, I—"

"Zack!" It was Ms. Spencer. She had followed him out into the hallway. Now she was walking quickly toward him.

"If you're lucky she'll give you a detention," Leo said in a low voice. He laughed and punched Zack on the arm as he took off. "Later!"

"Later," echoed Zack as he turned around to face Ms. Spencer.

"I'm glad I caught you, Zack," she said with a smile. She looked around. Then she said quietly, "Is your father Andrew Brown, the real estate agent?"

"Uh, yeah," Zack replied, surprised.

Ms. Spencer nodded, her blue eyes searching Zack's face. "I see. And how is he doing lately?"

Zack looked puzzled. "He's…fine, I guess." He paused and then asked, "Do you know my dad or something?"

Ms. Spencer gave him the same strange look as before. "Yes, actually, I do. He sold my house for me a few months ago."

Zack just nodded.

Ms. Spencer didn't say anything else. She seemed to be watching him very closely.

What's her problem? Zack wondered. "Um… Ms. Spencer? I'd better go. I'm going to be late for next class," he said.

She nodded. Then she said, "Be sure to do both parts of question six in tonight's homework." Then she walked back to her room.

That was weird, Zack thought. *Maybe she can just tell something is bothering me. She didn't ask me what's wrong, though.*

He was deep in thought as he walked through the halls to his locker. He hardly noticed when Heidi appeared.

"Hi!" she said, grabbing his hand. "I was looking for you this morning. I just saw Leo, and he said you came late. What happened?"

Zack frowned and looked away. "I didn't get much sleep last night," he said.

"Did you sleep in?" she asked.

They had reached Zack's locker. He stopped and began fiddling with the lock. "No...not really," he said. He didn't know where to begin explaining what had happened. And truthfully, he didn't know if he was ready to talk about it.

He changed the subject. "Hey, I was thinking maybe we could go to the Retro Dance on Friday night," Zack said.

Heidi looked confused. "What dance?"

"The one the student council is having," he explained. He stuffed his math books inside his locker. He pulled out his geography binder. "Jodi was putting up signs all over the school."

"Did you say Friday night?" asked Heidi. Zack nodded. "I can't go. I have to work," she said. "You should go with Leo."

"Yeah, maybe," said Zack. He wasn't really listening. In fact, the Retro Dance was the last thing on his mind.

They walked down the hallway together. Zack saw Michael standing in the middle of a group of grade nine students. They were taking turns signing his cast. Michael looked up as Zack and Heidi walked by, and he waved with his good arm.

"Hey, Zack! Come here for a second!" Michael called.

Zack stopped. "What?"

"Do you have soccer practice after school today?" Michael asked.

"No," said Zack.

"Can I get a ride home with you?" he asked.

"Sure, whatever," Zack said.

"I hope Mom's out of bed," Michael continued. "I really don't want to eat your cooking for supper."

Zack saw Heidi look at him, but he pretended not to see. "Yeah, me too. See you after school."

As they walked away, Heidi asked, "What's the matter with your mom?"

"She's sick," Zack said shortly.

Heidi stopped walking, forcing Zack to stop too. "Zack, what's up with you today? You're acting weird."

"Nothing!" Zack snapped. He saw the shocked look on Heidi's face and instantly felt bad. "Look, I'm sorry I yelled at you," he said. "I'm just having a bad day."

Heidi shot him an angry look. "Well, don't take it out on me."

They stood in silence for a moment, staring at each other.

"I have to go. I'll see you later," said Zack finally. He looked away from Heidi's face.

"Fine," said Heidi. She turned around and walked away.

Zack watched her go. Part of him felt terrible for being rude to Heidi. Part of him just wanted to be angry. Right then, he didn't care whose feelings he hurt.

chapter 13

common
denominator

The rest of the day passed in a blur. Lunch was awful. Zack had given his lunch money to Michael. He ate a stale chocolate bar that he found in his locker instead. Zack felt a huge sense of relief when the bell rang at three o'clock. He dumped his homework into his backpack and left the school as fast as he could.

He wasn't fast enough to get past Leo, though. "Dude!" Leo called over the heads of the students crowding the halls. "Wait up!"

Zack really wasn't in the mood to talk—not even to Leo. "I'm in a hurry, Leo," he said. He started walking again as soon as Leo caught up to him.

"That's cool. Hey, a bunch of the guys are going to Port Catherine Park to scrimmage tonight. Can you come?" Leo asked, falling into step beside Zack.

"Uh, no, I can't," Zack said. "I'm busy."

"Busy doing what?"

"Nothing," said Zack, an edge creeping into his voice. "Just forget it, Leo."

"What's your problem?" asked Leo, grabbing Zack's arm.

Zack stopped walking and jerked his arm away. "Lay off, will you?" he said angrily.

Leo stared at him. He shook his head and said, "Man, you're *wacked* today. Did you have a fight with Heidi or something?"

Zack whipped around. "My parents are splitting up!" he snapped. "There. Are you happy now?"

Leo's mouth dropped open. "No way. Are you serious?"

Zack started walking again but much more slowly. He started talking, more to himself than to Leo. "I just can't believe it...they've been married for, like, twenty years...how can they get divorced? I guess they have been fighting a lot lately, but..."

It all came pouring out. Zack told Leo about the fight that his parents had the night before. "I haven't talked to my dad," said Zack quietly. "Michael and Shellie don't know yet. My mom didn't even get out of bed this morning." He shook his head. "What a mess."

Leo nodded. "Yeah. It sucks," he said. "I mean, I was just a kid when my parents got divorced. I don't remember much about it. But my dad took it pretty hard."

Zack stared at him. He had forgotten that Leo's parents had split up when he was a kid. It had happened a long time ago. Zack hadn't even known Leo then. Leo's mom had remarried and moved up north with her new husband. Leo never saw her. She didn't even send birthday cards. Leo's dad had remarried, too. Jodi and Leo had lived with their dad and his new wife since they were little kids.

Zack took a deep breath. "Look, I didn't mean to…"

"Don't sweat it, Zack," Leo said, slapping him roughly on the shoulder. "What are friends for if you can't yell at them when life sucks?"

Zack gave a laugh. "Yeah, I guess."

They walked out to the parking lot in front of the school. "What happened when your parents got divorced, Leo?" asked Zack.

Leo shrugged. "I don't really remember much about it. I was only a kid. They sold the house. Jodi and I moved into a smaller place with my dad. My mom didn't want custody. She moved out of town with her new husband. I think they ended up having a couple of kids." He said all of this without a trace of bitterness.

Zack nodded, but his mind was spinning. He couldn't imagine his own parents getting remarried and having more kids. He could hardly even imagine his dad moving out of the house!

"Where is your dad now? Is he still at home?" Leo asked.

"Nope. He took off last night. He said he'd be back to pick up his stuff sometime," said Zack. He felt his stomach relax a little as he talked about it. Saying it all out loud was helping. Still, he hated the idea of telling the rest of his friends. They all had normal families. He felt a surge of anger at his dad for screwing everything up. *So much for being normal*, Zack thought angrily.

chapter 14

the bitter truth

All the way home, Zack worried about what was going to happen next. Whatever was happening at home, Zack was sure it wasn't good. *What if Dad is there right now, moving his stuff out? What if Mom and Dad are fighting again? What if Mom is still in bed? Am I supposed to cook dinner?* His stomach growled, reminding him that he'd missed lunch.

Michael started talking about soccer as soon as he got in the car. Zack hardly listened to a word his brother said. His mind was on other things. He stopped at a red light. Howard's Grocery Store was on the corner. It was busy at three-thirty in the afternoon. The parking lot was nearly full. Zack stared at the store for a few moments. He glanced at Michael. "Hey, Mike, I want to stop in here for a minute," he said. He pointed at Howard's.

"Why?" Michael asked.

"Because if Mom is still sick in bed, then we'll have to make supper. I think we should buy some cold cuts and buns. And we used all the milk at breakfast this morning," said Zack. In the back of his mind, he knew that he was just stalling. He really didn't want to go home yet.

Michael groaned. "Aw, man, are we having *sandwiches* for supper?"

"Do you want to cook?" asked Zack as he pulled into Howard's parking lot.

Michael just scowled.

Zack checked to make sure he had his bank card in his wallet and walked inside. He waved at a tall blond guy who was stacking cans of soup on a display.

"Hey, Kalen, how's it going?" he called. Kalen was a popular guy at Bayview High. They weren't exactly friends, but he was in a couple of Zack's classes.

Kalen looked up. He grinned at Zack. "Hey, Zack," he said.

Zack stopped next to a table piled high with fresh tomatoes. *Maybe we could make BLTs,* he thought. *I guess we'll need some bacon and lettuce, too. Would Shellie eat a BLT? Probably not.* He picked up a tomato and turned around to ask Michael. As he looked up, he saw something that almost made him drop it.

His dad was standing several feet away.

Zack's mouth fell open. He didn't know what to do. All he could think of was the look on his dad's face when he said that he wanted a divorce. Zack's heart began to pound loudly in his chest. *Did he see us? What should I do? Did Michael see him?*

Michael turned and looked in the direction that Zack was staring. He began to say, "Hey, what's Dad doing—"

Suddenly, a blond woman stepped close to Mr. Brown and put her hand on his shoulder. She leaned close to him and said something quietly in his ear. He laughed and turned to face her. Then he put an arm around her waist and kissed her.

Michael was frozen to the spot, staring at them. Zack couldn't believe his eyes. He shook his head. "But...what's he—who's he—is that *Ms. Spencer?*" he sputtered.

It *was* Ms. Spencer. She was still wearing the same red dress she had worn to school.

Michael suddenly came to life. He walked around the display of tomatoes, right up to his dad. "*Dad!* What are you *doing?*" he shouted.

Mr. Brown and Ms. Spencer jumped apart. They looked as though someone had thrown cold water on them. Mr. Brown's smile vanished as he looked down into the red, angry face of his middle child. "Michael, we should go somewhere and talk," said his father in a low voice. He glanced around and saw Zack, still standing there with a tomato in his hand.

Zack didn't need to hear his father's explanation. It was pretty obvious what was going on. You didn't have to be a genius to figure it out. His dad was fooling around behind his mom's back. With his teacher. Zack felt like he couldn't breathe.

This is impossible, he thought. *This can't be happening to me.*

"Let's go outside and talk, boys," Mr. Brown repeated, his voice still low and calm. He reached out to touch Michael's shoulder, but Michael jerked away from him.

"Don't touch me!" he shouted. "Who is *that?*" He pointed at Ms. Spencer, who was standing behind Mr. Brown. She looked like she wanted to disappear.

Other shoppers were watching them now. Zack walked over to stand with Michael. "Come on, Mike, let's go home," he said. He looked at his dad. "You remember what *home* is, right

Dad? Some of us still live there." His voice was cold. He didn't even look at Ms. Spencer. *I can't believe I liked her,* he thought. He felt sick.

Michael was shaking his head. "No. I want to know what's going on," he said firmly.

Mr. Brown set down his plastic basket. He turned around and said quietly to Ms. Spencer, "I need to talk to my kids, Amanda. I'll see you later." He didn't touch her or kiss her. She watched unhappily as he turned around and walked out.

Michael followed his father out of the store. Zack turned to go too, but he stopped when Ms. Spencer said, "Zack, I'm so sorry about this."

Zack stopped. He turned around to face her. She didn't seem pretty anymore. He had never hated someone so much in his whole life.

"How long have you been going out with my dad?" he spat at her, not caring who could hear him.

Ms. Spencer bit her lip. "Three months," she said finally. "But Zack, I never meant—"

"I just want to know *why,*" he said angrily. "Why did you...why *him?* He's my *dad!*"

"I didn't expect this to happen, Zack. I'm really sorry—"

"Just forget it!" Zack said in a choked voice. He turned and walked away as fast as he could.

Kalen Sommers was still stacking cans of soup nearby. Zack didn't look at him as he walked by. *Great*, he thought. *Kalen must have heard every word. Now everyone at school will know.* His heart hammered against his ribs. His head felt like it was going to explode.

He squinted in the bright sunlight and looked around. He saw his dad's SUV parked at the end of a row of cars. Michael and Mr. Brown were sitting inside.

Zack started walking toward them. His feet seemed to be made of stone. He didn't want to hear his father's explanation for this. There was no way to explain it, anyway. His dad was having an affair with his teacher. His parents were getting a divorce. Nothing his father could say would make a difference. As far as Zack was concerned, his life was ruined.

chapter 15

confession

Michael was sitting in the front seat of the SUV. His broken arm lay on his lap. He leaned his head on his right hand and stared sullenly out the window. Zack got into the back seat and slammed the door shut. He knew his father was looking at him. He kept his eyes on the back of Michael's seat.

Mr. Brown cleared his throat. "Boys, your mother and I have been having problems for a while now," he began.

"Oh, *really*? We hadn't noticed," Zack said. He couldn't keep the bitterness from his voice.

Mr. Brown ignored Zack's comment. He just went on talking. "I know you're both angry and upset right now. You have every reason to be mad at me. But I want you to understand that I love you guys and Shellie very much. Nothing will ever change that."

A heavy silence fell upon the car. No one said anything. Until now, the idea of divorce had seemed crazy. Zack hadn't really believed his parents would split up. But when he saw his dad standing there, kissing Ms. Spencer…that was serious. Zack felt sick to his stomach. He opened the car door and got out.

"Come on, Mike. Let's go," Zack said.

Michael seemed to be in a fog. He opened the door. He struggled to get out without leaning on his cast.

Mr. Brown leaned across the seat. "I know you both need some time to think about all of this. I'll come to the house soon to talk to you again. And Shellie, too," he said.

Zack couldn't bear to listen to his father any longer. He turned around and walked away without another word.

Michael began talking as soon as they got in the car. "I don't believe it! How could he do this?" he burst out. "Do you think Mom knows about that woman?"

Zack didn't reply. He stared straight ahead at the road.

Michael shot a quick look at him. "Did you know about this already?" he asked.

"No...not exactly," said Zack.

"What do you mean, 'not exactly'?"

"I found out about the divorce last night," Zack admitted. "But I didn't know Dad was...I didn't know about the rest of it until just now." He gripped the steering wheel tightly.

"Why didn't you tell me?" Michael asked.

"Because I didn't believe it!" Zack snapped.

They drove in silence for a few minutes. Suddenly Michael said, "So what's going to happen now?"

"I don't know," Zack muttered. "I don't think Mom knows that Dad has a *girlfriend*." He practically spat the word out.

"Should we tell her?" asked Michael.

Zack didn't answer. He turned the car onto their street. He felt a quick flash of panic. They were almost home. *How are we supposed to pretend we don't know anything?* he thought.

They parked the car in the garage, but they didn't get out right away. "What are we going to say to Mom?" Michael asked again.

"I don't know, Mike!" Zack snapped. "I'm thinking, okay?"

"Well, we'd better think of something," Michael said. He glared at Zack. "We can't exactly keep it a secret. She's going to find out sooner or later."

Zack didn't say anything. *Yeah, but do we have to be the ones to tell her? How am I supposed to tell my mom that my dad is having an affair with my teacher?* He sat for a few minutes, thinking. *I don't want Mom to find out from someone else. If she finds out we knew and we didn't tell her, she'll be even more mad.*

"I think we should tell her," Zack said finally.

Michael nodded. "Yeah. Me too."

The house was quiet and still. Zack and Michael went to the kitchen first. The breakfast dishes were no longer sitting in the sink. The empty cereal boxes were gone, too. *Mom must have cleaned up,* Zack thought. *So that means she got out of bed.* He just wasn't sure if that was a good thing or a bad thing. At least if she was still in bed, they wouldn't have to face her.

"Zack? Michael? Is that you?" called Mrs. Brown. "We're in the living room."

"What are we going to say to her?" whispered Michael.

"I don't know," Zack hissed back. "I'll think of something." *I hope,* he thought to himself.

Mrs. Brown was sitting on the sofa with Shellie. The television was turned off. Right away, Zack knew that they were talking about the divorce. Shellie's eyes were red and her cheeks were flushed, as though she had been crying. She was huddled next to her mother in a tight ball.

"Sit down," said Mrs. Brown. Her voice sounded tired and old. She had dark shadows under her eyes. Her curly hair wasn't combed.

Zack sat on the other sofa, but Michael wouldn't sit down. They waited for their mother to say something. She looked at each of them and started to talk but stopped. She sighed and looked up at the ceiling as if she were looking for help.

She took a deep breath and began. "I've been talking to Shellie about something. It's…it's about me and your dad."

"We already know," said Zack quietly. Michael glanced at him but didn't say anything.

Mrs. Brown looked surprised. "You do?" Zack just nodded. "Oh. Maybe you should tell me what you know," she said.

"We know about the big split," Michael blurted out.

Shellie looked up. "Don't say that, Michael," she said tearfully.

"Well, it's true! Isn't it, Mom?" said Michael. He seemed to be waiting for her to say that it wasn't true. That it was all just a big mistake.

But Mrs. Brown nodded and said in a hollow voice, "Yes, it's true. Your dad and I are getting a divorce." Tears welled up in her eyes and spilled down her cheeks. She hugged Shellie closer.

Hearing his mother say it made it painfully real. Zack felt tears in his own eyes. He looked quickly at the floor.

"Mom, doesn't Daddy love us anymore?" whispered Shellie.

"Of course he does," said Mrs. Brown, wiping at her eyes. She looked over at Zack. "Come here," she said, patting the empty space next to her. Zack didn't move.

"I just want to know why," Zack said.

Mrs. Brown nodded again. "I know, Zack. I...I wish I could tell you. I guess people just change. They don't want the same things anymore..." her voice trailed off helplessly.

Michael said suddenly, "Mom, we know what's going on! We saw—"

"Let's go into the kitchen," Mrs. Brown said quickly. "I want to make a cup of tea. Shellie, sweetie, go and wash your face, okay? Do you want me to make a cup of hot chocolate for you?" Shellie gave a slight nod. She went slowly upstairs to the bathroom, sniffling.

Zack and Michael followed their mother to the kitchen. "Mom—" Zack began, but his mother cut him off.

"Tell me what you saw," she said quietly. "And keep your voices down."

So Zack told her what happened at the grocery store. Mrs. Brown listened without saying a word. Her face seemed to be carved from stone. She didn't cry or yell or anything.

When Zack finished, she said, "I'm sorry you saw that." Her voice was tight with anger.

Zack narrowed his eyes. "Did you already know that Dad was having an affair?" he asked.

His mother closed her eyes and took a deep breath. Then she looked him straight in the eye. "Yes," she said. "But Shellie doesn't know, and I absolutely *do not* want you to tell her. This is hard enough for her to understand. Do you hear me?"

Zack and Michael nodded.

"And no matter what happens...I love you very much," said their mother. Her voice shook a little. "Nothing will ever change that. You can come to me any time to talk about *anything*, okay?" She put her arms around both of them and pulled them together for a hug.

Later, Zack was in his room, trying to do his homework. He was just sitting there, staring at the page, when his mom knocked on the door. She looked in and said, "Can I come in?"

"Sure," said Zack.

She sat down on the edge of Michael's bed. "Where is your brother?" she asked.

Zack shrugged. "I think he's watching TV."

His mother nodded. "I wanted to talk to you privately, Zack. I'm sorry about this morning. I just…I couldn't face all of you." She looked into Zack's eyes. "Are you angry with me?"

"No," Zack mumbled. He looked down at the top of his desk. "Well, I was a bit mad this morning, but I'm not now."

Mrs. Brown smiled a little. "It's hard being the mom, isn't it?"

"Yeah," said Zack. He glanced up. "Hey, Mom, can I ask you something?"

"Of course," she said.

"Why didn't you leave Dad when you found out about…everything?" he asked. He watched her face carefully.

Mrs. Brown considered his question for a moment. "Well, I guess I didn't want to believe it at first," she said slowly. "I thought we could work it out together."

"But Dad didn't want to?" asked Zack. It hurt to talk about it, but he just had to know.

His mom sighed. "Well, honey, I think your father just knew that it wasn't something he could work out. He doesn't want to be married anymore." The words came out in a painful whisper. Suddenly Zack was sorry he had asked. He looked away from his mom's face. He didn't know what else to say.

Mrs. Brown said softly, "It's going to be hard for all of us, Zack. But it's going to be all right. You know you can talk to me any time. No matter what your father does, or what he says." Her voice was hard and angry for a moment. She curled her hands into fists and she closed her eyes for a second. "Okay?" she said quietly.

Zack just nodded, unable to speak.

His mother came over and gave him a hug. Zack held back his tears until she had gone. Then he climbed into bed and turned out the light. It took him a long, long time to fall asleep.

chapter 16

friends and enemies

Zack walked into math class on Wednesday morning filled with dread. *How am I supposed to sit there and act normal with Ms. Spencer now?* He considered skipping out of class. He couldn't skip math for a week until Mr. O'Grady came back, though. *Might as well get it over with,* he thought grimly.

Ms. Spencer wasn't there yet when he walked into class. He realized that he was holding his breath, and he let it out in a whoosh. He took his seat in front of Leo.

"Hey, man, I thought you were coming over last night. Where were you?" asked Leo.

Zack turned around. "It's a long story," he said in a low voice. "I'll tell you later."

"Come on, what happened?" Leo pressed.

Zack looked around. No one was paying any attention to them. They were all talking and laughing loudly. He said, "Remember what I told you about my parents?"

"Yeah," said Leo.

"Well, yesterday I saw my dad kissing Ms. Spencer," Zack whispered.

"WHAT?" Leo cried. A couple of people stopped talking and looked over.

"*Shhhhh!*" Zack hissed.

"Are you *serious?* That's crazy," said Leo. His eyes were wide with disbelief.

"Yeah," said Zack darkly.

Suddenly, they heard the classroom door shut. Zack's shoulders dropped. It was the moment he had been dreading.

"Good morning, class," said a deep voice. A short black man stood at the front of the room, holding a stack of papers. "My name is Mr. Jamieson. I'm filling in for Mr. O'Grady for the rest of the week."

Zack's mouth hung open for a second. *She isn't coming back.* The thought brought a sense of relief, and he relaxed a little. At least he didn't have to deal with Ms. Spencer at school. What about outside school, though? Was his dad serious about Ms. Spencer? Would his dad expect him to hang out with him and his new…girlfriend? The thought made Zack grind his teeth together. *No way*, he thought to himself. His mind began to race. *What if they get married? What if they have kids together? Please don't let that happen*, he prayed silently. He spent the rest of the period deep in thought.

When the bell rang, Zack gathered his books and left. Leo was close behind him. Once they were outside, Leo said, "Whoa! I guess Ms. Spencer is lying low now. Her dirty little secret is out in the open." He sighed. "That sucks. She *was* pretty."

"Watch it, Leo," Zack growled at him.

Leo held up his hands and said, "Okay, okay. I was just kidding."

Zack said nothing. He was just glad he didn't have to sit through two more days of math class with that woman. As they walked around the corner toward their lockers, Zack saw Heidi standing there waiting for him. She didn't look happy.

"Listen, I've got a spare now, so I'll catch you later," said Leo.

"Later," said Zack. He walked over to Heidi. He felt bad about yelling at her yesterday. He just didn't want to talk about his stupid family anymore.

"Hi," he said, trying to smile.

"Hi," Heidi said. She didn't smile back. She brushed back her hair with one hand and waited for him to talk.

Zack sighed. "Look, Heidi, I'm really sorry I was a jerk yesterday. It's just that things are messed up at home right now..." He told her about the divorce.

"Oh, Zack...I'm so sorry...I didn't know..." Heidi's green eyes were wide with shock. She reached up and hugged him.

"It's okay," Zack said. It was weird. He felt awful every time he talked about it. But he felt a little bit better at the same time.

They walked down the hall to their next class. Zack thought, *I guess I have to tell people sooner or later.* He cringed when he thought of Kalen Sommers standing there in Howard's. *He must think I'm a freak,* Zack thought.

Later that day, Zack was getting changed into his gym clothes. He had just pulled his T-shirt over his head when Kalen came into the boys' change room. He was already dressed in his gym shorts and shirt. Zack tried to act like everything was normal. "Hey, Kalen," he said. "How's it going?"

"It's cool," said Kalen. "Hey, Zack, I'm sorry to hear about your mom and dad. My buddy Scott went through the same thing. His mom cheated on his dad. She wasn't dating a teacher, but..." he stopped suddenly. He looked a bit uncomfortable.

Zack bent down to tie his shoelaces. "Yeah, well, thanks Kalen," he muttered. *Great. So people do this all the time. Is that supposed to make me feel better?* he thought.

"Well, Scott's parents stayed together. It was pretty weird at their house for a while, but it's okay now," said Kalen. "Maybe your parents will work it out, too." He smiled and went out.

Zack knew Kalen was just trying to make him feel better. He also knew, deep down, that his parents were not going to stay together. It was over, just like his dad said.

chapter 17

just one dance

By Friday, Zack's dad still had not come over to the house. *Where do fathers go when they move out all of a sudden? Maybe hotels have special rates for people who leave their families,* Zack thought.

Leo wanted to go to the Retro Dance at school. Zack wasn't in the mood. But Leo finally talked him into it. They decided to go, just for a little while. Heidi couldn't get the night off from the Donut Man, so it was just the two of them.

Michael wasn't going to the dance. He had been spending a lot of time at home lately. He stopped going out with his teammates after his soccer practice. He hardly went to Patrick's house. At first Zack figured it was because he was depressed about the divorce. Michael wasn't in a bad mood, though. He was more helpful than he had ever been in his life. He offered to clean up the dishes after dinner. He even helped Shellie with her homework. Mike was acting like a different kid. It was a little weird. It was a lot better than being miserable, though.

Zack and Leo arrived at Bayview around eight o'clock. Music blared from the gym. Here and there, lava lamps glowed and shifted into weird shapes. A huge, silver disco ball twinkled overhead. Zack and Leo walked through a curtain of beads into the gym.

"Cool," said Leo. He handed his ticket to a girl dressed in a tie-dyed dress.

Leo's outfit was wild. He wore a shiny, lime-green shirt with a wide collar. Several fake gold chains hung around his neck. Gold rings covered his fingers. He had on tight polyester pants. The best part of his costume was a huge, curly wig. People stared at him as he strolled in the door. A few girls laughed and pointed. Leo didn't care. He loved the attention.

"I think I've seen that wig before...wait, doesn't it go with your clown suit?" said Zack with a laugh.

Leo laughed back at him. "Like you can talk...where did you get those crazy shoes?" he asked, pointing at Zack's feet.

A trip to the local used-clothing store had turned up all sorts of retro clothes. Zack even managed to find a pair of platform shoes. They were dark purple vinyl. The soles were at least three inches thick.

"What? You don't think they look *groovy* with this suit?" Zack pretended to brush lint off his powder-blue suit. It practically glowed in the darkened room. The pants were a little too short. They just added to the whole cheesy effect of his outfit.

"Hey, guys! Great outfits," called a girl's voice. Zack turned around and saw Jodi walking toward them. His jaw dropped.

Jodi looked stunning. She wore a purple minidress that showed off her legs. Zack noticed that it barely covered her rear end. Even her makeup looked retro. Her eyes were lined with thick black eyeliner, and her lips were shiny and pink.

She walked over to Zack and Leo, grinning up at them. "Nice hair, Leo," she said.

"Thanks," said Leo, patting his Afro.

"You did a great job with the decorations, Jodi. I can hardly tell it's the old Bayview gym under all this stuff," said Zack.

"Thanks!" said Jodi, flashing a warm smile at him. "I'm glad you came, Zack."

"Where's the food?" Leo asked.

"There isn't any, moron," Jodi said. She rolled her eyes. "Is that all you think about?"

The DJ began to play "Stayin' Alive." As if on cue, the dance floor was flooded with people. Leo began to walk toward the dancers. "Are you two coming?" he called over his shoulder.

"Nah. Maybe later," said Zack.

Jodi looked Zack up and down and whistled. "Cool costume," she said.

"Thanks," said Zack. His mind was wandering back to the scene at home. *Maybe I shouldn't have come tonight,* he thought. He tried to push thoughts of his parents out of his mind.

Jodi didn't ask him about his parents. *I wonder if Leo told her about it,* Zack thought. In a way, he was glad she hadn't asked him about it. It was a relief not to talk about the divorce.

A slow song from the old *Grease* movie began to play. People were pairing up on the dance floor. Zack saw Leo's Afro swaying above the heads of the other dancers. Suddenly, Jodi grabbed his hand and said, "Hey, let's dance to this one."

Zack frowned. "Um, Jodi…I'm not really…"

"Come *on*," she pleaded, tugging on his arm. "Just one song, Zack. Please?"

With a sigh, Zack said, "All right."

The lights of the disco ball swirled around them. Zack slipped his arms around Jodi's waist. He tried not to think about his father, but he couldn't help it. He pictured his dad standing in the produce aisle at Howard's. He imagined his dad's arm around Ms. Spencer. *Just stop it*, he told himself, squeezing his eyes shut. *Say something to Jodi.* He tried to think of something interesting. His brain felt foggy.

Jodi looked up at him. "Zack, you should loosen up. You feel as stiff as a board." She leaned a little closer. "I *love* this old song," she said, swaying in time with the music.

Zack tried to relax his shoulders a little. The top of Jodi's head barely reached his chin. He could smell her hair. It smelled fresh, like green grass. He took a deep breath.

"That's better," Jodi murmured against his chest. The room was dark and warm, and Zack felt like he was hardly moving. Slowly, he began to relax.

Jodi was singing the words of the song softly. Her fingers tapped gently on his collar to the beat of the music. "Hopelessly de-vo-ted to youuuuu…" she sang.

The song was almost over, but Zack hardly noticed. Jodi pulled away from him a little so that she could look at him.

"Thanks for the dance," she said.

"Sure. No problem," Zack replied, smiling back. He actually felt a little better. The song was over. They still stood with their arms around each other, though.

Jodi seemed to read his mind. "I think you needed a hug," she teased. "You're actually smiling now. You looked so mad when you first got here."

Zack gave a short laugh. "Oh, really?"

"Yeah," said Jodi, grinning at him. Then her face became serious. "You're a great guy, Zack. Do you know that?"

"Uh…thanks," he said.

Then she closed her eyes, leaned forward and kissed him.

At first, Zack was too surprised to do anything. A single thought passed through his head: *This feels good.* Then his brain realized what his body was doing. He pulled back and stared at Jodi in shock.

"ZACK!"

He whipped around. Heidi was standing right behind him.

chapter 18

caught!

Zack stepped away from Jodi. "Heidi! What are you doing here? I thought you had to work," said Zack, trying to think of what to say.

"So you thought you'd pick up somebody else tonight?" Heidi shot back. A few of her friends were standing with her. They all glared at Zack.

"This isn't what you think!" he blurted.

Heidi narrowed her eyes. Her gaze darted to Jodi and back to Zack. "Oh, really? Because I think you're *cheating* on me! *With Leo's sister!*" she shouted.

People were beginning to stare at them. They stopped talking and began to listen.

Zack was filled with panic. He had to make Heidi understand. He walked toward her and left Jodi standing by herself. "Heidi, I swear, I didn't do anything—"

Zack felt himself being shoved very hard, and he fell backward onto the floor. A few people gasped and moved out of the way. Zack looked up into Leo's angry face.

"What do you think you're doing with my sister?" he shouted.

Zack got to his feet quickly, which wasn't easy in vinyl platform shoes. "Look," he said, trying to sound calm, "I didn't touch your sister. We were just dancing—"

"Yeah, right," one of Heidi's friends said. "It didn't look like 'just dancing' to me."

Heidi's eyes began to fill with tears. "Zack, how could you?" she said. She shook her head and began to walk away.

"No! Heidi, wait!" Zack grabbed her arm. She stopped and threw off his hand, glaring at him with disgust.

"Don't touch me!" she shouted. "You're just like your *father!*" She stormed out of the gym.

Zack stopped as if he had been slapped. His heart was pounding, and he felt like he was having a terrible dream. *This can't be happening,* he thought numbly.

He became aware of the sudden silence in the gym. The entire school was watching him and Heidi. Leo was still standing there, looking like he was ready to punch him in the face. Jodi was gone. Zack had never felt so alone in his whole life.

"Zack. Hey, Zack. Wake up."

Zack was lying on his bed, face down on his pillow. He opened his eyes. Michael was standing there, shaking him by the shoulder. Zack groaned and rolled over. All he wanted to do was stay in bed. For the rest of his life.

"Go away," he muttered. He turned his face away from Michael.

Michael poked him again. "Come on, Zack. Wake up," he said again.

"I said go *away!*" Zack growled, throwing a pillow at Michael. It nearly hit his broken arm.

"Hey! You almost hit my cast, loser!" said Michael. He picked up the pillow and threw it back at Zack, hitting him on the back of the head. Then he stomped out of the room, slamming the door behind him.

Zack didn't move. He felt terrible. He had tossed and turned all night. When he did sleep, he dreamed that he was running through the halls of Bayview High. He was trying to get out, but all the doors were locked. He kept waking up sweating and out of breath.

The memory of the school dance was still fresh and painful, like an open wound. He felt guilty for kissing Jodi. The worst part was, even though he didn't mean to do it, he couldn't deny that he had enjoyed it. That made him feel even more guilty. *That was a pretty stupid thing to do*, he thought. *Everybody saw us. They probably think I'm a total jerk.* He knew at least two people who thought so: Heidi and Leo.

Every time he closed his eyes, he saw the hurt look on Heidi's face. After she walked out, he had wasted no time in leaving, too. He hadn't wanted to stick around after she yelled at him. Her words still stung: *You're just like your father. How could she say that? In front of the entire school?* he thought.

Okay, I know I messed up. But that was a low blow, he thought.

Zack lay in bed for a little longer. Heidi's words nagged at him. *What if I am just like my dad?* he wondered. People often said he was the spitting image of his dad. They looked and talked alike. Even the way they laughed sounded similar. *But that doesn't mean I'm exactly like him*, he thought. *Even if I did kind of cheat on Heidi.* He hated to admit it, but it did seem like he was acting like his dad. Finally, he rolled out of bed.

His mom was sitting at the kitchen table when he went downstairs. She was sipping a cup of coffee. She looked up when he came in.

"Good morning," she said. "You got home early last night. I didn't think you'd be home from the dance until after midnight."

"I didn't feel like staying all night. It was boring," Zack said. In his head, he thought, *Oh, except for the part where I kissed my best friend's little sister. And I had a screaming fight with my girlfriend in front of the entire school.* He tried not to think about it. *There's nothing I can do about it now,* he told himself. *What's done is done.*

He poured himself a glass of orange juice. Then he stuffed a couple of frozen waffles in the toaster. He stared gloomily out the window over the sink. The sky was gray. Dark clouds were gathering quickly overhead.

Mrs. Brown stood up and walked over to the sink. "Looks like rain," she remarked. "They're calling for thunderstorms today." She rinsed out her cup and looked sideways at Zack. "So, what are your plans for today?" she asked.

"I don't know," said Zack. "I guess I'll just hang out." He couldn't call Heidi or Leo after what had happened last night. *They probably won't even talk to me,* he thought. *Maybe I'll just go back to bed.*

His mother folded her arms across her chest and looked out the window. She seemed uptight about something. "Your dad is coming over today," she said. She didn't look at Zack as she said it.

The waffles popped up. Zack looked over at his mom, but she was still looking out the window. Her face looked tense. "When?" he asked. He put the waffles on a plate and went to fridge to get the maple syrup.

"Around eleven o'clock," his mother said. "Are you okay with that?"

Zack shrugged. He squeezed syrup onto his waffles. "Yeah, I guess so. Does Michael know?" he asked.

She sighed deeply. "Yes. He was pretty upset about it. He said he doesn't want to talk to Dad. I let him go over to Patrick's house to calm down," Mrs. Brown said.

"Well, I don't feel like talking to Dad either," Zack said, frowning. "But I guess I'll have to eventually, right?"

"That's up to you, Zack," his mom said.

"What else am I supposed to do? Ignore him forever? Pretend he doesn't exist?" Zack asked.

"You have to decide what kind of relationship you want to have with him," said his mom. "You don't have to figure it out right away, Zack. Just think about it." She squeezed his shoulder and then walked away.

Zack sat down at the table to eat his breakfast, but he no longer felt hungry. He poked at his waffles. He tried to ignore the nervous feeling in the pit of his stomach. *Great. My life just gets worse and worse. Why does he have to come today?* He knew he had to talk to his dad sooner or later. There was nothing he could do about it.

He thought about what his mom had said. *I have to decide what kind of relationship I want to have with him. Well, what if I don't want one at all?* Zack thought. He pushed his waffles around with his fork. *He's never around, anyway.*

Thunder rumbled outside. Zack looked up and saw the first raindrops hitting the window. The storm was on its way.

chapter 19

a father's love

Zack was lying on the sofa and reading a comic book when he heard a car outside. *That must be Dad*, he thought. He sat up. His shoulders slumped forward and he let out a heavy sigh. *May as well get it over with.*

His mother was sitting at the kitchen table. Her laptop computer hummed in front of her. She glanced at Zack and said, "I think you should go outside to see your dad." She picked up a steaming mug of tea and took a sip.

"Why?" Zack asked.

His mother set down her mug with a thump. "Because I don't want him to come in the house," his mother said. "He's not picking up any of his things. He's just coming to see you kids. He doesn't need to come inside." She pressed her lips together. She was trying to sound calm, but there was an edge in her voice.

She doesn't want to see him, Zack realized. *I guess I can understand that.* "Okay, Mom," he said. He got up and went to the front door.

The air outside was damp and warm. Mr. Brown was just stepping out of his car. "Hi, Zack," he said. He seemed unsure of himself—something Zack wasn't used to. His dad was always so sure of himself. He was always in control.

He's nervous because of me, Zack realized. *He doesn't know what to say.* Somehow, this thought made Zack relax slightly.

"Hi, Dad," he said. His throat seemed tight and dry. He cleared it loudly.

Mr. Brown smiled again, but his eyes looked sad. "I'm sorry I couldn't come by sooner. I've just been busy."

"Whatever," muttered Zack. He looked away and rolled his eyes. *Figures,* he thought. *He takes off in the middle of the night without even saying good-bye. Then he's too busy to come and talk to us for a week. What a jerk.*

"Where are Michael and Shellie?" Mr. Brown asked.

"Shellie's here. Mike went over to Patrick's house," Zack said.

That made his dad frown. "Michael isn't here?" he said.

"DAD!" shouted a voice. It was Shellie. She was standing just outside the door. She ran toward him with a big smile.

Mr. Brown picked her up and hugged her tightly. "Hello, sunshine!" he said. "How's my big girl?"

"I miss you, Dad," said Shellie, her voice muffled in his shoulder.

"I miss you, too, honey," said Mr. Brown. His voice was full of emotion. Very gently, he put her down. He looked into her eyes and said, "Shellie, I'm going to spend all afternoon with you. Right now I need to talk to Zack. Okay?"

"Okay," Shellie nodded. She went back to the house. At the door, she stopped and looked back once before going inside.

Zack looked down at the ground. Neither he nor his dad broke the silence for a few minutes. "Why don't we go for a drive?" Mr. Brown finally said.

"Okay," said Zack with a shrug.

It was a quiet ride. Zack didn't know what to say. *He should say something first*, he thought angrily. *I'm not the one who took off and fooled around behind Mom's back.* He suddenly thought about kissing Jodi at the dance. *Well, I guess I'm not totally innocent. But that has nothing to do with this situation.*

"How's school?" asked his dad.

"Fine."

Silence.

"I heard you played a good game against Lincoln last week," said Mr. Brown.

"Yeah."

They drove on. The silence became louder than words. *Say what you came here to say!* Zack wanted to shout. He clenched his fists and fought the urge to yell at his father.

There was a coffee shop on the next corner. "How about a coffee or something?" his dad asked, pointing ahead.

"Whatever," said Zack. Mr. Brown pulled into the coffee shop and parked the car. Zack jumped out and slammed the door. Rain pelted down on his head. He walked quickly into the coffee shop ahead of his dad.

When they were both sitting down with drinks, Mr. Brown took a deep breath. Then he said, "Zack, I need to apologize to you."

That's the understatement of the year, Zack thought. He chewed his straw and said nothing. He stared out the window. The rain was coming down harder. It hammered against the pavement and the cars outside.

Mr. Brown kept talking. "I'm sorry I left the way I did. I'm not proud of my actions over the past few months. I know I've been selfish, and I didn't mean to hurt you. I love all of you very, very much."

Zack looked his dad in the eye and shook his head. "Well, you sure have a funny way of showing it," he said coldly.

Mr. Brown stared hard at Zack. "No matter what happens, I still love you," he said firmly.

Zack looked away again. A coffee grinder buzzed loudly behind him. In spite of the air conditioning, the room felt much too warm to Zack. He could feel his face beginning to turn red. He closed his eyes and resisted the urge to punch his dad in the face.

chapter 20

a time for truth

"**W**hy did you do it, Dad?" Zack demanded, looking his dad right in the eye.

Mr. Brown cleared his throat. "I don't know. I guess I just…I didn't think about what would happen when I…when I met Amanda. It just…happened. I didn't mean to hurt anyone." He looked so uncomfortable. For a minute Zack wondered if he might bolt out of there.

"Yeah," said Zack. He cringed at the mention of Ms. Spencer's name. He hated the way his dad called her "Amanda." He remembered the day Ms. Spencer found out his name. No wonder she acted so weird when she talked to him.

Zack stared at his dad. "She's a lot younger than you, isn't she?" he accused.

"She's twenty-nine," said Mr. Brown.

"Did you know she was my teacher?"

"No, not until this week," said his dad. "I knew she was a supply teacher, of course. She usually works at private schools. There was only a slight chance that she could end up teaching you. She forgot that you were a student at Bayview High when she took the job there. When she found out that you were in the class, she left."

"Yeah, that was really nice of her," said Zack bitterly. "Tell her I said thanks."

"Look, Zack, I know how you must feel—" his dad began.

"NO YOU DON'T!" yelled Zack. A few people turned to look, but Zack didn't care. All of his anger burst out of him at once. "You don't know how I feel about anything! You haven't been around for months. And now I know why! You're a liar and a cheater, and you...you *suck* as a dad!" He jumped up from the table.

Mr. Brown stood up too. Zack had his father's height and his broad shoulders. They glared at each other, their noses level. At that moment, they looked more alike than ever.

"Zack," his father said sternly, "I know you're upset right now. But I expect you to treat me with respect."

"Respect? You want *respect?*" said Zack in disbelief. "How can you expect me to *respect* you when you're treating us all like crap?" He turned around and stormed out of the coffee shop. He shoved open the door as hard as he could on his way out.

The pavement was wet and slick from the rain. The air felt cool and fresh against Zack's hot, flushed face. He walked to his father's car, his heart drumming against his rib cage. He was breathing hard, as though he had been running. He wanted to pound something. He paced around the car.

The sound of his father's footsteps made him look up. Mr. Brown came toward Zack and stopped a few feet away. Zack glared at him. Neither of them said anything.

Finally Mr. Brown spoke. "Zack, I came to talk to you today because you're my son. Think whatever you want about me. But my kids are more important to me than anything else in the world. Even if you hate me right now." He stopped and cleared his throat. "I don't expect you to forgive me right away. But I hope you can, someday." His voice cracked a little and he swallowed hard.

Zack ran one hand through his thick, blond hair. In a way, it would have been easier if his dad had just left. It was painful to hear him asking for forgiveness like this. It made him seem so sad. Zack couldn't really look at his dad's face. If he did, he knew he would start to cry. He coughed and rubbed his eyes. "Yeah, okay," he muttered.

His father moved toward the car. "Are you ready to go home?"

Zack nodded. "Yeah, but I'm going to walk," he said.

"Are you sure?" his dad asked. His eyes were full of worry.

"Yeah, I'm sure," Zack said. *Just leave me alone*, he thought.

His dad nodded. "Okay. I'll call you tonight," he said. He got in the car. With a last wave, he drove away.

Zack watched until his dad's car was out of sight. Overhead, the sky was clearing up. The storm was moving on.

chapter 21

clear conscience

The only thing worse than talking to his dad was calling Heidi. Zack put it off as long as possible. He was too mentally tired to do it on Saturday. By Sunday afternoon, he knew he had to call her. He waited until Michael and Shellie and his mom were outside. Then he dialed Heidi's number, held his breath, and waited.

"Hello?" said a woman's voice.

Oh, great. It's her mom. "Um...Mrs. Taylor? It's Zack."

"Oh, hello, Zack." Mrs. Taylor's voice turned frosty.

"Could I please talk to Heidi?" Zack asked.

There was a small pause. "Yes. Just a moment, please." Zack heard a small click as Heidi's mom put down the phone.

A minute later, Heidi picked it up. "Hello?" she said. Her voice sounded small and sad. Zack was flooded with guilt. *I am such a jerk,* he thought to himself.

He cleared his throat. "Heidi, it's me. Zack. I, uh...I wanted to call you and say I'm sorry. I feel terrible about what happened at the dance. I was a total idiot. I never meant to—I mean, I'm sorry I hurt you," he said quietly.

Dead silence.

"Uh, Heidi? Are you there?"

"Yeah."

"Did you hear what I said?" Zack asked.

"Yeah."

"So, um, can we—I was wondering if we could start over?" Zack asked hopefully.

"I don't know, Zack," said Heidi. Her voice trembled a little.

"Heidi, I'm really sorry," Zack said softly. "I swear I'll never do anything like that again."

Zack heard Heidi sigh deeply on the other end. "I don't know, Zack. You really screwed up. I can't trust you. You went behind my back."

Zack's heart crashed into his stomach. *She's dumping me,* he thought.

"I just need some time to think about things," said Heidi. Her voice sounded a bit stronger. "I think we need some space."

"Sure," Zack said. He didn't know what else to say.

"Hey, Zack," Heidi said.

"Yeah?"

"I'm sorry about what I said. About you being just like your dad. I was just mad," said Heidi. "I didn't mean it."

"Oh. Sure. Don't worry about it," said Zack. "I deserved it, anyway."

"Bye, Zack."

"Bye." Zack hung up the phone and went upstairs. He threw himself onto his bed and stared up at the ceiling. *Well, this is officially the worst weekend of my entire life. My parents are splitting up. My girlfriend is probably going to dump me, and my best friend hates me.* Zack closed his eyes and tried not to think about it.

THWACK!

Something struck his windowsill. "What the heck..." Zack jumped up. *It must be Michael and his friends acting stupid,* he thought. He walked over and opened the window.

Leo was standing down below. He was holding a soccer ball.

"What are you doing?" shouted Zack.

"Come on, dude! Hurry up!" Leo yelled.

Zack stared at him, totally confused. "Why? What's going on?" he asked.

Leo pointed at his bike, which was lying on the front lawn. His fishing rod and tackle box were strapped to the handlebars. "Fishing," he said simply.

A grin spread over Zack's face. "Right. Fishing," he said. He shut the window and ran downstairs to the front door. He'd thought Leo was going to kill him for kissing Jodi. *At least I can count on Leo*, he thought. *He must have decided it's not worth losing our friendship. It was just one stupid mistake.*

Zack pulled on his lucky baseball cap and opened the front door. As he stepped onto the front porch, he saw Leo's face right in front of him. The next thing he knew, he felt something hard connect with his stomach. Zack doubled over, gasping for air.

"What...did...you...h-hit me...for?" Zack wheezed. He clutched his stomach and tried to stand up straight.

"Dude, I couldn't let you fool around with Jodi and get away with it," said Leo. "She's my kid sister, after all." He grinned. "I feel a lot better now."

Zack's face was beet red. "Oh, good. That's good," he said, straightening up. "Look, Leo—"

"Don't even try to say you're sorry," Leo said. "It's over. I talked to Jodi about it. She said she's the one who kissed you. She feels pretty stupid about it. Did you talk to Heidi?"

Zack nodded. "Yeah. She's still mad. I don't know what's going to happen," he admitted.

Leo gave a snort of laughter. "You're lucky she didn't dump you right away. Now grab your gear. Let's go to the Peaks before it gets too hot." He turned around to get his bike.

Zack got his fishing gear and his bike from the garage. The boys began biking out to the river. The warm June breeze felt good rushing through Zack's hair. The sun beat down on the back of his neck. In spite of everything, he felt a little better. He didn't know what was going to happen next. He didn't know if Heidi would forgive him. But for the first time in days, he felt normal. *Whatever 'normal' is*, he thought as he pedaled hard up a hill.

glossary

Afro
A bushy hairstyle

apologize
To say sorry or express regret

conference
A meeting

custody
A relationship in which one person is
responsible for another person

flirting
To show romantic interest in another person

infection
A disease

pharmacy
A drugstore

polyester
A manmade fabric

retro
Describing a style of clothes, music, or culture
that was popular in the past

scarves (scarf)
A soft piece of cloth that is usually worn
around the neck

scrimmage
A practice game of soccer or another sport

señora
A Spanish word meaning "Mrs."

vinyl
A strong plastic material

Special Thanks

I would like to thank the talented women of Tea Leaf Press for devoting their time and energy to this book: Jane Lewis, April Fast, Kate Calder, and Hannelore Sotzek.

Thanks also to my husband John, whose constant support and encouragement keep me going.

A big thank you to Ben Kooter and Vanwell Publishing!